LOUIS XIV

Hasso Ebeling International

Contents

The Years of Development and Waiting

Childhood

Louis Dieudonné, first-born of Louis XIII, King of France, and of Anne of Austria, sister of Philip IV of Spain was born at Saint-Germain-en-Laye on 5th September, 1638. The two names given to the Dauphin when he was christened take us straight-away into the very heart of history. The first name because it was traditional in the long and glorious dynasty of the Capetians, and the second one even more so, because it was often used as a patronymic for offspring whose fathers were unknown. Thus, not even the fatherhood of the greatest monarch of all times escaped doubts and insinuations. It was indeed public knowledge that for quite some time the relations of the royal couple had been very cold.

Anne of Austria, daughter of Philip III of Habsburg, King of Spain, had been given in marriage when she was barely thirteen to the thirteen-year-old Louis XIII. The young girl, beautiful and full of life, was badly matched with a man as colourless and in such habitually poor health as Louis XIII. No wonder, then that the young bride should look for other entertainment: her affair with the brilliant and charming Duke of Buckingham, the English Ambassador to Paris, caused some scandal, although not too much by the standards of the day.

Although the king was "understanding", after some time he began to harbour a strong resentment towards his wife. Furthermore, the Queen also attracted the implacable hostility of Cardinal Richelieu, who was perhaps, as rumour had it, jealous of Buckingham, but who was certainly irritated by the damage that her lack of scruples was causing to the image of the monarchy he was trying to foster.

It was only during the last few years that the Queen was reconciled to her husband and then in a very cold and formal manner. The fruit of the reconciliation was indeed the birth of the Dauphin. There is an anecdote which goes as far as pinpointing the date of conception. On the evening of 5th December, 1637 the King went to visit his protégé, Sister Louise Angelique,

On a visit to the hospital of the Hôtel-Dieu, Louis XIII is accompanied by the Duc de Bellegarde, the Marquis de Souvré, and the Comte de la Meilleraye. He meets Mademoiselle de La Fayette, who is caring for the sick helped by the Sisters of Saint Vincent. This print represents the meeting of the Sovereign and the young girl, who is certainly not aware of the role that chance would attribute to her in the birth of Louis XIV.

Page 7:
Louis XIV, more the "son of discord" than the "Gift of God", shows even at the age of ten, in the expression of his face and his whole attitude, the signs of precocious maturity, which his situation as a child-king and the troubles of the time imposed on him. This painting is by Henri Testelin, the Court painter.

Mademoiselle de La Fayette, in a convent in Paris. According to the scheduled programme, this should have been followed by an overnight stay at the castle of the Condé family outside Paris. Since the conversation was very prolonged and, in the meantime, a dreadful storm had broken out (in December?), the commander of the royal escort advised the King to spend the night at the nearby palace of the Louvre, which was the residence of the Queen. The King accepted this change of plan without enthusiasm. It was precisely nine months later that the future Louis XIV came into the world. The uncanny "punctuality" of the birth and the need to explain the circumstances in detail, together with other royal intrigues which we shall mention later, inspired doubts, even in a great historian like Michelet: "The origins of great things are not always clear". The delivery was very difficult. During the first years of marriage the Queen had had two miscarriages and the memory of these increased the Court's anxiety. The King, without mincing his words ordered that the child should be saved "whatever happens". In the event, the delivery

turned out happily for both mother and child. Dieudonné was the name chosen by the King to show his thankfulness for the son for whom he had hardly dared to hope. The baby was healthy and plump with fine, regular features. As a matter of course his upbringing was in the hands of "the women", that is to say, the Queen and her court. This observation would be entirely trivial, except that it is relevant to the personality of the little prince. There is very little information on the earliest infancy of Louis, though some general indications can be clearly seen. Spoilt and pampered by "the women", he began to cultivate that egocentricity which was to become the strongest and most constant trait of his personality. It was certainly "the women" who instilled in him the first "poisons" against his father and against Richelieu, whose presence terrorised him.

The King loved having his son at his side, but the little Prince whimpered and wished to go back to "the women". It was only after much effort that he became accustomed to spending short periods of the day with his father, who was always serious and frowning. This probably resulted in the development of another trait of his character: the ability to conceal his own feelings.

On 4th December, 1642, Cardinal Richelieu suddenly died, even in this taking his enemies by surprise. The little Dauphin, who had approached the Cardinal as little as possible and always with a kind of fascinated terror, must have enjoyed a great sense of liberation. Straightaway, a veiled struggle broke out around the weak and sickly person of Louis XIII. The Cardinal had earned himself many enemies. His politics, which were oriented to a strong and centralised "modern" state built on the foundations of the Bourbon monarchy, had hit the nobility severely. As soon as news came that the King had a new illness which was thought to be fatal, all those who had been exiled or banished from the court, gathered against orders around the neighbourhood of Saint-Germain-en-Laye, the King's residence. They were headed by the young Duc de Beaufort, François de Vendôme, the illegitimate descendant of Henri IV, who had been exiled by Richelieu for taking part in the plot against him, led by the young Marquis de Cinq-Mars. At the bedside of the ailing King they behaved with so much arrogance that they gained themselves the nickname of *Les Importants*.

The King, before losing clarity of mind and aware of the dangers that threatened the succession, put his initials to a new will which he got Parliament to register (a formality which all acts had to undergo to give them effect as laws). But, influenced on the one hand by the wish to strengthen the monarchy and, on the other hand, by a mixture of fear and anger towards the Spanish inclination of his wife, his decision was ambiguous. He nominated Anne to be Regent and guardian of their sons until they came of age (a second son, Philippe, was born in 1640), at the same time reducing her powers almost to nothing by setting up a governing council to decide affairs of state by majority decision.

Louis XIII, son of the great Henri IV and of Marie de Medici, died aged forty-two, on 14th May 1643. There were few regrets. Certainly there were none on the part of his wife, but there were none either from his young heir (there is no trace of them in his memoirs). This no doubt, was partly because Louis was still very young, but mainly because the umbilical cord still bound him to his

Cold, wilful, clever, tenacious and subtle – these characteristics are very evident in the portrait of Cardinal Richelieu left to us by Philippe de Champaigne. Richelieu was the real master of political life during the reign of Louis XIII. At his death, barely a few months before the King's, he had laid the foundations for absolute monarchy. Such a monarchy was realised in a magnificent and unequalled manner by Louis XIV.

mother. However, that may be, the Dauphin quickly had to find a substitute for the image of his father in another great person.

That same day, as tradition has it, Anne of Austria officially assumed the Regency. Her first decisions were marked by an extreme prudence. She was wise enough to put aside not only her personal bitternesses, but also her family links with the Habsburgs, deciding on a policy of continuity and reinforcement of the monarchy.

Les Importants thought that power was theirs. Anne was firmly resolved to assert her rights, even opposing the decree of her dead husband. She knew very well how to hide her secret decision in order not to arouse any suspicion and she proceeded by degrees. As early as 18th May, she named as prime minister the most prestigious of Richelieu's associates. Cardinal Giulio Raimondo Mazzarini (Mazarin for the purposes of history, with only one "z", which is how he signed his name).

A stroke of good luck helped the Queen to carry this out almost unnoticed: from the field of battle came the news that the young Duc d'Enghien, the future *Grand Condé,* had won a crushing victory over the Spanish at Rocroi. France had been engaged in war against the Spanish and Austrian Habsburgs for some time, a war which came to be called the Thirty Years War. The people of Paris, rejoicing, saw this as a good omen for the government of the "good Regent".

For his part, Mazarin did not wait for the help of fate, proud as he was of being *faber fortunae suae* or master of his own fate. He had learnt quickly at Richelieu's school, though it was also in his own character, to conceal his personal ambitions very carefully under an affable and open manner. The image that we have of him at this time is that of a man who is rather modest in his words and deeds, generous, hospitable and with a seductive personality. Nothing about him warns of his later firmness.

Nevertheless, in the paths of history, weight can occasionally be given to reasons which are not wholly rational. "You will like him, he is like the Duke of Buckingham!", Richelieu had declared with rancorous insolence, before presenting his new associate to the Queen in 1632.

The tender feeling which united, and must have united up to the end, the Queen and Mazarin was not only the fruit of a rumour. The proof of this lies in the close correspondence which took place between the two, partly even before the King's death. The Queen even sent Mazarin two amorous notes that very day. Doubt only remains about the fact, maintained by some historians, that their liaison was belatedly legitimised by a secret marriage.

Anne's second step was to obtain from Parliament the annulment of Louis XIII's decree concerning the succession. She played skilfully on the ambitions of this institution (but it should be remembered that she was always supported by Mazarin's advice). The French Parliament had only the name in common with the English Parliament. Its functions were exclusively judicial and administrative, but it wished to gain greater powers of decision and government. The council which the dead King had wanted, in order to offset the apparent weakness of the Queen, presented itself as the main obstacle to achieving these ambitions. Only too late did Parliament realise that in invalidating the Royal will it had made Mazarin the true master of France. From then on, the latter disposed of powers which even Richelieu never had. This was one cause of the conflicts and plots which troubled France during Anne of Austria's Regency. The King, aged five (he was in theory King on the day of his father's death), was present at all these events. In the official ceremonies, he accompanied his mother, who diplomatically took him along as "justification" for her powers.

All the great historians of this period agree that, behind the demands of Parliament, the aristocracy and even the Third Estate, there was no precise political plan or any "political consciousness". At the very most, it was a question of certain classes or factions wanting to claim the largest share of power and riches that they could achieve. None of these forces could, however, declare themselves anti-monarchist, even indirectly. The idea of the monarchy, hereditary and with divine right, existing for the projection and sublimation of paternal power, was the true "unifying force" of the French people, and of its cultural and ethical-religious values. And the Queen made use of this "force" like a shield and received in return authority and prestige. The little Louis saw, as it were, through the eyes of his mother; so it is not surprising that he felt profound respect and real affection for Mazarin.

Opposite page:
Anne of Austria, here represented with the little Louis XIV in a picture from the French school of the time, revealed resources of character in her maturity which had not been suspected in her earlier years as Queen. With the constant support of Mazarin, she effectively succeeded in defending the interests of the child-king, despite the dramatic events which threatened the very presence of the Bourbons on the throne.

The Frondes

The "game" did not turn out to be easy either for the Queen or Mazarin. Periods of regency in the kingdom of France had always been the prelude to fights and upheavals. *Les Importants,* for their part, had been premature in counting on the influence they had with the Queen, who in Richelieu's time had joined their ranks to support the policy of peace with Spain. But Mazarin forced the hand of the Queen.

He was far-seeing and a real politician, who against all appearances believed in the plan inherited from his great predecessor. He therefore opposed, with absolute firmness, any sort of disengagement from the war and all offers of collaboration from Beaufort and his associates. *Les Importants* began to understand with whom they had to deal. They started to treat him haughtily and went as far as offending the Queen in public. Mazarin lost no time. With the pretext of a real or supposed plot against him, he had Beaufort imprisoned and the other opponents exiled, at the same time forming around himself a ministry made up exclusively of trustworthy followers. All this had already taken place by September, 1643, only a few months after the death of Louis XIII.

Les Importants were not the only ones to be surprised by the change of regime and to remain disappointed by it. Above all, the expectations of the French people were disappointed. They had hoped that the new state of affairs would forebode peace. Their condition was anything but flourishing and they found the very idea of continuing the war effort insufferable. It would mean, in particular, new tax burdens, which were already very heavy for the peasants and the artisans, the only productive classes; the clergy, the aristocracy and the state officials were, by contrast, almost exempt from tax impositions. The discontent with the government of Mazarin also increased for another reason. The Superintendent-General of Finances, Jacques André d'Emery, was Italian and so the suspicion, artfully spread by Parliament, that there was a foreign plot to bleed France, found increasing credit. The tension among the people would not perhaps have brought about serious consequences (although numerous *jacqueries,* or peasant revolts, took place in the provinces) had Parliament not decided to use it as a weapon to foster its own plan. We have already mentioned the ambitions of this institution; it was formed for the most part of nobles *de robe,* who drew considerable proceeds from their office and who aspired to the acquisition of legislative powers and, in particular, to the control of the State finances. The office (and the noble title attached to it, which gave the right to wear the *robe*) was hereditary and like all the other administrative offices was bought at great expense through the famous *paulette,* a particular tax which at the time of Henri IV had taken its name from its creator, Charles Paulet. It gave to the members of Parliament a certain security of tenure and their arrogance matched it. Richelieu had kept them rigidly at bay, reducing their powers, mindful of the Fronde, which they had unleashed under the regency of Marie de Medici. Now they were trying to do the same again. During the first few months of 1644, they opened hostilities: Parliament formally resolved not to register any more acts dealing with finances or taxation. Mazarin underestimated their strength. He thought he would be able to act as he had done with *Les Importants* and

Pierre Mignard, *Portrait of Cardinal Mazarin.* Mazarin was far-seeing, a real politician, and he believed, against all appearances, in the great plan he had inherited from his predecessor. He opposed with absolute firmness all forms of disengagement from the war against Spain and all offers of alliance from Beaufort and his group.

he had the president and three councillors thrown into jail. Parliament's reply was unanimous. For three months it ceased to perform any judicial acts and Mazarin was forced to yield and free the detainees.

It was a serious defeat. The victory it had won rekindled Parliament's ambitions and the Cardinal had to call on all his resources as an astute negotiator to tame Parliament and obtain its approval to new taxes, which were indispensable for the continuation of the war.

Mazarin had lost face and with it his good manners. He had become reserved and discourteous. He was generous only in corruption and made up for his weakness with a network of dependants. He was hated by the powerful, whom the people gladly supported and with whom they sang *Mazarinades,* lampoons on Mazarin, partly composed spontaneously and partly spread by Scarron, a poet and story-teller. In the meantime, echoes of these tensions were reaching Louis through the anxieties of his mother and her long conversations with Mazarin, which he often witnessed. The events of 1648

remained in his memory for a long time. During January that year, while Mazarin was patiently pursuing his strategies, which resulted in the Peace of Westphalia, open warfare by Parliament against the crown broke out. This was going to be the last war of the old independent powers against the institution of monarchical absolutism. Once again Mazarin had trodden too heavily in expecting to subject the judicial and administrative officers to a special tax. The result was to push the other great departments of state, like the superintendents of finances, the court of finances and the Great Council to make common cause with Parliament. The coalition was very united and belligerent, and went so far as having some confused notions about "reforming the state". The Royal Court in turn was in such financial difficulties that the Regent was forced to yield to all the demands of Parliament.

The coalition set up some sort of dictatorship. It deposed Superintendent-General d'Emery, appointed a commission with the task of checking all the accounts of the public finances and abolished all those taxes which had not been

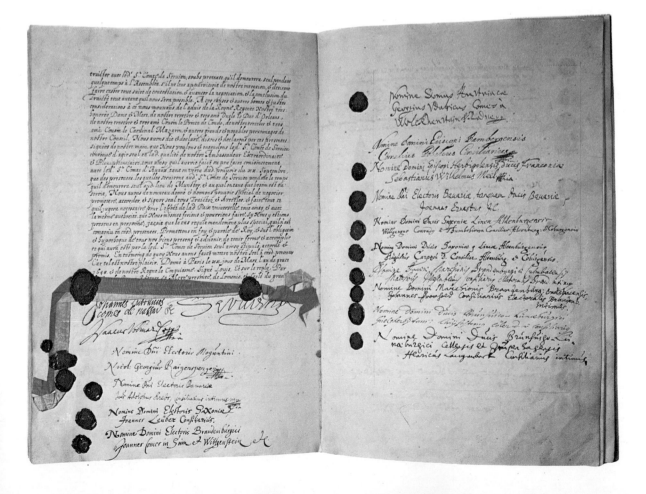

The Peace of Westphalia was concluded in 1648 at Münster and Osnabrück, between the German Emperor, France and Sweden. It put an end to the Thirty Years War. Mazarin reaped the fruits of the intervention against Austria decided by Richelieu. The reproduction shows the last two pages of the peace treaty.

The Encounter of Brie-Comte-Robert, an episode in the blockade of Paris of 1649, represented by the painter Sauveur Le Conte. Frightened by the return of the Grand Condé from the war front at the head of part of his troops, Parliament declared a state of siege; the town was therefore attacked by the victor of Rocroi.

freely approved by Parliament itself. The rebellion could have had some very serious results. Seeking to appease the assembly, the Regent once more had recourse to the young King. The latter was almost ten, tall and slender, but still carrying the marks of smallpox from which he had recovered with difficulty a few months before. He affected a dignified and respectful attitude, but already knew well enough that this assembly was his main enemy. In his presence, arguments ceased and only simple administrative acts were carried out, but as soon as he left, confrontations broke out again more fiercely than before.

The Court was drawn into an extremely difficult situation: the insubordination and the usurpation of powers by Parliament seemed irrepressible.

The unexpected announcement of a new great victory by Condé at Lens on 20th August, 1648, reversed the course of things. On this occasion they say that the King made the comment: "The gentlemen of Parliament are going to be very angry". Thinking the moment had come to counter-attack, the Regent imprisoned the body's president Blancmesnil and the old councillor Pierre Broussel, a very popular personality. It was

another serious mistake: immediately, the town was covered with barricades and the few troops were pushed back into their quarters. Parliament had Paris in its hands. It demanded that the prisoners be freed and, fearing an attack from Condé, who had returned slightly wounded from the battlefront with some troops, declared a state of siege. The Regent had to make new concessions and even the Peace of Westphalia, signed on 24th October, did not bring the Court significant advantages. In fact, the war with Spain continued to be waged.

Mazarin, pre-occupied with the peace negotiations, kept relatively in the background during these last events. He even suggested to the Queen that she should make a semblance of abandoning her point-of-view and encourage people to foresee the possibility of a change of government. Condé at this time had the unfortunate idea of frightening Paris with ostentatious preparations for a siege. Tension grew to the point of inspiring fears for the safety of the Royal family. On the night of 5th January, 1649, Louis and Philippe were transported to Saint-Germain-en-Laye. Was this flight really necessary? The anguish and the fright that the young Sovereign experienced sowed the seeds, as he himself admitted, of all his future acts of vengeance against Parliament.

The situation developed brutally. At the announcement of the King's flight, Paris took up arms again. On 8th January, Parliament banished Mazarin, that "disturber of public order, enemy of the King and of the State". At the head of the revolt were certain nobles, of whom many, such as the brother of the great Condé, were related to the Royal family, and who had been harshly hit by Richelieu's policies and now again by those of Mazarin. The intervention of these "lords, ready to slit each other's throats", as Cardinal de Retz wrote, caused the downfall of the Fronde. As Voltaire says, each made pacts with the other, each betrayed the other and each treated on his own account with the Royal house. The people quickly wearied of fighting for the courtiers without receiving anything from them, and went back to their normal occupations. Moreover, operations were led on both sides without conviction or resolve, due to lack of ideas and serious motivation. Negotiations started which resulted on 1st April in the Peace of Rueil.

The treaty gave an amnesty to the rebels, on condition that they "loaned" twelve million *livres* to the crown. There was no question of the expulsion of the "foreigners", the main request of Parliament, which then realised what it had given up at the negotiating table. The only clear outcome was the personal profits made by certain great nobles.

Mazarin, who had patiently stayed to one side, experienced a wicked pleasure in seeing everyone turn against Condé, because of his equivocal conduct during the whole affair. He decided to profit by it: he attracted to his support the most influential man of the Fronde, an unreliable but very cunning personality by the name of Paul de Gondi, the future Cardinal de Retz, promising him no less than a cardinal's hat. The latter unleashed all parties against Condé, who with his brother and others was imprisoned in the chateau of Vincennes on 18th January, 1650.

Mazarin seemed to have triumphed, but the situation was still very confused: the Spanish had entered into Picardy, then into Champagne; in Guyenne, Condé's friends had risen in revolt; numerous provincial parliaments had evicted the King's governors. Paul de Gondi, not seeing his

“The Prince of Condé, to whom the State owes its glory and the Cardinal his safety, puts his services at too high a price and becomes a rebel because of his pretensions”. So runs the inscription on this print of the time explaining the transfer of the Grand Condé to prison at Vincennes, together with his brother the Prince of Conti and the Duc de Longueville. “He was determined to get himself arrested”.

cardinal's purple shining on the horizon, rapidly made a new about-turn: he allied himself to Gaston d'Orléans, brother of Louis XIII and therefore uncle of Louis XIV. It is hard to say what were his real intentions (or those of the great Condé). Was his plan to dethrone his nephew? That this idea had crossed his mind cannot be ruled out, but his immediate objective was probably to take Mazarin's place in the government.

From now on the young King clearly understood the game of the various factions and knew that from a wider viewpoint he was himself the stake in it. He followed events with a precocious maturity and appeared more and more often in public ceremonies. It was a period of anguish and uncertainty and the plots woven by persons of his own blood must have removed any remaining illusions he may have had about human nature. At this point, new fears were born from events in England. In January, the news of the execution of Charles I, uncle of Louis XIV, had sent a shudder of horror throughout France. One evening, the Parisian mob, wanting to reassure itself of the King's good health, had the palace gates opened and they filed through his bedroom all night long while he pretended to be asleep.

The struggle broke out again with ferocity. In February 1651, strengthened by the support of the Duc d'Orléans and of the Fronde of the Princes, Parliament asked the Queen to dismiss Mazarin and release the princes from captivity. Mazarin considered it prudent to travel in all haste to Normandy. This time the Queen was forced to give her approval and Mazarin had to leave France. He settled not very far away, in Brühl, near Cologne, from where he could easily follow the course of events.

The Queen herself and her children were practically held prisoner. Condé, having regained his freedom, put himself at the head of the Fronde, but this led to yet another about-turn on the part of Gaston d'Orléans, who for the time being supported the Queen. Profoundly disgusted, Condé left Paris to recruit an army of his own on 7th September, 1651, two days after Louis had

The third child of Henri IV and Maria de Medici, Gaston d'Orléans, shown here in a portrait of the French school of the eighteenth century, was one of the main personages of the Fronde of the Princes. More fortunate than Condé, he was by the will of Mazarin relegated to the castle of Blois.

entered his fourteenth year and officially came of age. For all practical purposes, power remained in the hands of his mother, who from then on acquired the additional advantage of being able to make official use of the name of the King.

The young monarch, however, also began to make personal use of his own authority. He started a journey to the south-west of France to attempt, by means of his own presence, to bring the rebels and Condé himself to reason. Condé was in the process of recruiting his army in that area. As soon as the Court had left Paris, thereby escaping Parliament's surveillance, the King wrote a message in his own hand to Mazarin telling him to return to France secretly.

In February, 1652, Mazarin took the road to Paris at the head of six thousand soldiers who were wearing the green livery of his house, thereby defying Parliament. The King went to meet him with the entire Court and, after a year of absence, Mazarin returned in great triumph. Perhaps in order not to oppose their Sovereign's specific wish, Parliament did not take any counter-measures, but the same group of princes who had earlier opposed the Queen and Mazarin, with predictably Gaston d'Orléans at their head, did. Paul de Gondi, who had finally become Cardinal de Retz, kept himself to one side.

Having collected an army, Gaston occupied Anjou, attracted the Spaniards to France, and negotiated with Condé for a common line of action. The Vicomte de Turenne, after many changes of side (he had also been with the Spanish), finally gave his support to the King.

It looked like civil war: France was divided by flags of different colours – blue (Orléans), red (Spain), Isabella white (Condé) on the one side; white and green (Bourbon and Mazarin) on the other. But the *entente* within the coalition was more apparent than real. By clever manoeuvring, Turenne forced Condé to take refuge in Paris, then having penetrated the Saint-Antoine quarter with a larger army, he chased Condé from house to house as far as the Bastille. Gaston did not move to help Condé. Instead it was his young daughter, Anne-Marie-Louise, Duchesse de Montpensier, who put herself at the head of part of her father's army and rushed to Condé's support. According to the legend, it was she who protected Condé's retreat by drawing the first fire of the Bastille. "That cannon fire killed her husband", was Mazarin's later comment, for until that moment, Anne-Marie-Louise, cousin of the King, had been the likeliest candidate to become Queen of France.

Having saved Condé, whose men were very hard pressed by then, the Duchesse also tried to persuade Parliament to take sides against the Court, but its members were wavering. The Parisian mob renewed any hesitation, however, by celebrating the disagreements amongst the powerful factions in their usual way by taking to the streets and rioting. Partly motivated by genuine enthusiasm for *la Grande Mademoiselle,* as they immediately nicknamed the Duchesse de Montpensier, and partly because they really hoped for a change for the better, the *canaille* forced Parliament and the town council to declare themselves against the King, by means of a violent riot. A further proof that Parliament never intended direct opposition to the institution of monarchy can be found in the fact that on this occasion a considerable proportion of its members fled from the city and set up a counter-parliament in Pontoise. Mazarin, for his part, aware that the situation was evolving in his favour and to speed up events, left France again during August and withdrew to Bouillon.

His calculation proved correct. His departure removed the rebels' incisiveness and *les grands,* more discordant than ever and without any political objective, remained inert. This delay was all to the Court's advantage. Numerous delegations were sent to the King to persuade him to go back to the capital, but the reply was always the same: those responsible for the disorders must leave first.

Condé, tired and disheartened, left Paris on 13th October to go to Spanish Netherlands. The victor of Rocroi and Lens passed into the service of the King of Spain, in the capacity of a *generalissimo* who was never esteemed. Shortly afterwards, the Duc d'Orléans retired from the scene as well.

Another episode in the Fronde of the Princes, in a painting of the French school of the time: fierce fighting under the walls of the Bastille in the Saint-Antoine quarter.

Consolidation of the Monarchy

On 21st October, the King and his Court triumphantly entered Paris, joyfully welcomed by the fickle crowd. The monarchy, or at least the dynasty, had been genuinely threatened: perhaps a man of the moment had been lacking. Condé was no politician and Gaston d'Orléans was manifestly mediocre. Finally, Parliament's objectives were typically feudal and thus anachronistic. The only basic element in the situation was the exasperation shared by all social classes, who were trapped between the last jerking motions of a feudal world, which was disintegrating and obscure longings for a new world, which could not as yet be clearly seen. In this context, the monarchy was still the only secure point of reference and therefore it could not help winning. The project of Richelieu and Mazarin of a "rational state", centred on the monarchy, endowed with an efficient bureaucracy directly controlled by the government, besides being the only project which could realistically be pursued, was also the only political project worthy of the name.

The young King had adopted it and made it his own in all its essential points. The first measure of the "new era" was that those principally responsible for the Fronde should "remain exiled" in their own domains. As for Cardinal de Retz, he was imprisoned at Vincennes, the first of many candidates for the role of that "man in the iron mask", whom we shall mention later.

The measures did not provoke counter-measures which promised well for the future. Mazarin left Bouillon and, on 3rd February, 1653, he returned to Paris for good. Yet again, the King went to meet him with the Court and all the more eminent people in the town had to pay homage to him, whether they liked it or not. Immediately, the Cardinal began the task of re-ordering the state. He formed a ministry of "vile bourgeois", as Saint-Simon was to say later on, but its members were active and capable and among them were Colbert and the elder Le Tellier, who were to become ministers of the Sovereign in the future. Having stifled the riots and restored internal order and peace, Mazarin had to look to the conduct of the war. The neglected French armies had been pushed back from Italy, from the Pyrenees and from the Netherlands.

In November, 1653, the King appeared at the head of his army to infuse the soldiers with courage and a fighting spirit, but he kept at a safe distance from the enemy.

His solemn coronation was celebrated with a grandiose ceremony in Rheims cathedral on 7th June, 1654. The feasting and celebrations were beyond description. Thus, the "orchestration of consensus" around the Royal figure began.

With the Court and the person of the King himself at the centre of so many events, little time had been devoted to the systematic education of the young Sovereign. All we know of his first five years, up to the death of his father, is that he was looked after by "experts".

The carousels, composed of manoeuvres and parades and performed by horsemen of the Court, were among the spectacles preferred by the organisers of the festivities of Louis XIV. The engraver, Israel Silvestre, has left us a wonderful representation of the festival of 1662 (detail of the left side: horsemen filing by in the lists).

After many unsatisfactory trials, the choice of tutor fell on the Abbé Hardouin Beaumont de Péréfixe, the future Archbishop of Paris, who lavished all his knowledge and goodwill on his pupil, but with scanty results. In his memoirs, Louis openly admitted that he had not been a model pupil: study was painful to him and did not arouse his interest. With the instinctive sensitivity of children, he must have found the precepts of his patient teacher somewhat abstract and out of keeping with the pressure of events. His education was through experience and by providing him with the key to interpret this experience, his real teachers were his mother and, particularly from 1653 until the time of his death, Mazarin. From Mazarin he gradually learned the art of ruling men, the use of subtle diplomacy, the ability to play on the rivalries and weaknesses of others. "This is demonstrated", writes Robert Mandrou, "by the deference and patience with which he waited for the cardinal's death before taking power into his own hands, by the care he took in surrounding himself with his own creatures, by the subtle camouflage which appears in certain lines of conduct".

In this same period, the young Sovereign also received his emotional education. He was sixteen, but appeared twenty. As he frequented Mazarin's house and Mazarin, like a good Sicilian, had brought his relatives and friends to France, he was attracted to the Mancini sisters one by one. His interest fell first of all on Olympe, the eldest, but she did not take him seriously. In 1657, she married Prince Eugène of Savoy, who was created Comte de Soissons; she is remembered in particular for having given birth to Prince Eugène, the famous General. Only much later was she going to bestow on the King those favours she had denied him as a young girl.

The King also courted Hortense, the most beautiful of the Mancini sisters, but his choice was finally fixed on the third, Marie. It was a genuine infatuation; Louis was speaking in terms of marriage. Mazarin, however, intervened very firmly, since he had very different plans. He abruptly sent his niece away and explicitly forbade her to correspond with the King. In 1661, Marie became the bride of Prince Colonna (in whose household Mazarin had done his apprenticeship and who was later to become viceroy of Aragon and of Naples).

Disputes developed in the family and words which were less than regal flew about, but Louis's devotion to the Cardinal and affection for his mother finally prevailed. Apart from the pains of the unfortunate love affair, he was deeply wounded and Marie's indignant reproof "You cry and you are King" remained with him for a long time. Mazarin had set a high example in showing that he could subordinate the interests of his own family to those of the State, but for the young Sovereign the experience was full of anguish and it was probably fatal in determining his future relationships with the gentle sex. Having cast aside his "real love", the road to a long series of "courtesan loves" was open.

From left to right: Olympe, Hortense and Marie Mancini portrayed by an unknown artist. Renouncing Marie was a terrible test for the young King and probably fatal for his future relations with the gentle sex: having cast aside his "real" love, the road was open to a long series of courtly affairs.

The Peace of the Pyrenees

In the meantime, the fortunes of war were beginning to favour the French. An Anglo-French army, commanded by Turenne, had made its way into the Spanish Netherlands. On 14th June, 1657, the Spanish army, commanded by Don John of Austria with Condé at his side, was totally destroyed on the dunes near Dunkirk. All Spain could do was to start negotiations. After preliminary approaches, these were conducted in a spectacular manner by the two prime ministers, Don Luis de Haro for Spain and Mazarin for France. Reasons of prestige and protocol did not allow either of the two powers to negotiate in a position of apparent inferiority. A stratagem had to be devised.

The Bidassoa is a river which flows from the Pyrenees towards the Bay of Biscay. Part of its lower course marked the border between the two states. Here, the solution of so many insurmountable diplomatic difficulties was to be found in a little island known as the Isle of the Pheasants, which was in neutral territory. It was here that, after crossing two bridges thrown from the opposing banks, the delegations and the respective Courts met. After more than forty years, Queen Anne of Habsburg was meeting her brother Philip again. The Spaniards, all indistinguishably dressed in black with white starched collars, were affecting a very haughty manner; the French were more colourful and distinguished themselves by their noisy and frivolous manner.

It was here that, on 7th November, 1659, what was to be called the Peace of the Pyrenees was signed. It was an important treaty in French history and also in the personal life of the King, since it agreed his marriage to his cousin, the Infanta Marie-Thérèse of Habsburg, daughter of Philip IV. The negotiations had been difficult and the marriage presented many sticking points, particularly the clause by which the future bride (and therefore Louis) was made to renounce all rights to the Spanish crown.

The other difficulty, a "point of honour" with the Spaniards, concerned the pardon and reinstatement of Condé. Astutely, Mazarin concluded by yielding almost entirely to the requests of his counterpart. They were, after all, purely formal, and ensured for France a number of concrete advantages: the southern frontier was pushed

back to the natural line of the Pyrenees and that of the north was reinforced by part of Artois and by Luxembourg, not to mention many advantageous gains in southern Flanders.

Moreover, on the "point of honour", Condé was certainly pardoned, but it was the Spanish who had to cede him a countdom in Flanders whilst the King allowed him to return to his properties in Guyenne in the following year. On the other hand, the French renunciation of rights to the

throne of Spain cost the Spanish the fabulous dowry of half a million *thalers-or.*

Mazarin knew that rich as Spain was, she would not be in a position to pay such a sum in ready money and that the non-discharge of the debt would fully restore the King's rights to the Spanish throne. During the Summer of that year, the Cardinal had formed the League of the Rhine (Mainz, Trier, Cologne, Hesse and Bavaria), as part of the Peace of Westphalia. This assured France a power of intervention in the German sector. Jan De Witt, Stadholder of Holland, the traditional enemy of Spain, rallied his policies to the French cause. Furthermore, thanks to the threatening intervention of Mazarin, the Peace of Oliva was hurriedly concluded on 3rd May, 1660, to the advantage of Charles X of Sweden. It is a measure of the power that France had acquired that she was able to do this for one of her allies even when he was in a losing position.

In a Europe at peace and with France never having attained such prestige since the time of Henri IV, the marriage of the King to the Infanta of Spain was celebrated, by proxy in Spain on 3rd June, 1660. Six days later the marriage was properly solemnized in France. It was preceded and followed by celebrations and popular festivities.

Love matches are not always possible for Kings. However, Louis conceived a tender affection for his bride, which was to survive the first regal distractions. At the time of his great loves, she kept to one side with dignity and without dramas, and the King in his own way remained grateful to her. The laconic Royal "epitaph" for her death in 1683 was: "This is the only displeasure she ever caused me". But an even more important event was about to change the life of the young Sovereign: the decease of Mazarin.

The Cardinal died, in a totally unexpected manner, on 9th March, 1661, at the age of fifty-nine. He was born in Pescina, a small town in Abruzzo, where his father Pietro Mazzarini, a Sicilian, administered the landholdings of the Colonna family.

He finished his studies in the Roman college of the Jesuits and in 1622 gained a degree in *utroque jure,* but he was never ordained a priest. Instead, it was as a captain of infantry that he entered the Papal service. During the first war of Montferrat, he acted as a mediator between the Habsburgs, the Savoyards and France, during which time he met Richelieu (the first meeting took place at Lyons on 9th January, 1630). Richelieu immediately appreciated the diplomatic qualities of the young captain. Mazarin remained for a few more years in the service of the Pope, Urban VIII Barberini, and he worked towards the Peace of Cherasco between Piedmont and France. In 1632, he took minor orders to be able to benefit from an ecclesiastical endowment from St. John-in-Lateran administered by France. From that moment on, although formally depending on the Vatican, he acted as Richelieu's direct emissary. In 1635, he was nominated a nuncio extraordinary to Paris, in 1639 he received French citizenship and in 1641 he was made a cardinal. It was Richelieu himself who recommended him to Louis XIII as his successor.

He did not have the political genius of Richelieu nor his decisiveness, nor his impetuosity, but the results of his work were even more impressive. He had a calculating nature and was reluctant to confront problems directly. He preferred to outflank them, flow with events and direct them from a distance by means of small corrections, without ever losing sight of the end. Patience, tenacity, lack of prejudices and an incomparable acumen

This detail of a tapestry designed by H. Testelin, represents the wedding of Louis XIV to Marie-Thérèse. The bride was not what one could call a beauty, but she did not lack charm: small, slender and well-proportioned, she had long wavy pale blonde hair and beautiful pale blue eyes. Her lips, on the other hand, were thin and determined, a "characteristic" of the Habsburgs.

in spotting the weaknesses of adversaries were his greatest qualities.

In this he was, without any doubt, the real teacher of Louis XIV. His final political master-stroke (from the point of view of monarchy and absolutism) was the battle he conducted against the Jansenists, who appeared to undermine the authority of the State and the religious unity among the educated Parisian class, though they did not seem to have much effect among the people at large. He had the "five theses", which were the foundation of their thought, condemned by the Sorbonne. Their doctrine could only appear dangerous calling, as it did, for moral vigour and coherence whilst refusing all manner of compromise and tolerance. He had the *Lettres provinciales* of Pascal publicly burnt (fortunately for the author they had been published anonymously) and he persecuted and dispersed the movement's disciples.

As one might imagine, he left an enormous amount of wealth, the fruit of honest gains. He had arrived in France with little but his own luggage. Apart from the considerable salaries that he received for the many positions he held, he annexed the profits from the direct government of Alsace, Breisach, La Rochelle, Brouage and Philippsburg, and he enjoyed the revenues of two archduchies, various counties and of forty of the richest abbeys of the kingdom. He also appropriated enormous sums from the State coffers, and sold public offices for his own profit.

In 1660, whether to save his own soul, to preserve his reputation for posterity or for some other obscure reason (always, however, determined by a definite political design), Mazarin had created the College of the Four Nations. This was founded to provide instruction for the young people of the newly-acquired frontier provinces (that is to say, Spaniards from the Roussillon and Cerdagne provinces, Walloons from the Low Countries, Alsatians and Piedmontese). It may not be right to express moral judgements at so great a distance, but the historian cannot help noticing the ambiguous results of Jesuit morality and of the Counter Reformation in the life of Mazarin who was exemplary in his time. In any event, the wealth accumulated by the Cardinal turned out to be useful to the young Sovereign. Whether it was as a memory to relieve the grief caused by his loss or as a "legitimate inheritance", it was suspected that the King took over a great part of his valuables and pictures and also a sum which amounted to several millions in cash.

He probably learnt on this occasion the final, fundamental lesson of his great master: power becomes rooted and strengthened to a large extent by means of what we now call "status symbols". One can already see the rising of the Sun King. If there is any purpose in studying the development of the King's personality, it is that it allows us to understand what was for contemporaries and many historians alike, the cause of great surprise. Just one day after Mazarin's funeral, Louis addressed the following words to the incredulous ministers whom he had urgently convoked, "Gentlemen, I gathered you to tell you that up until now I have been happy with letting the Cardinal take care of my business, but the time has come for me to govern myself. You shall help me with your advice when I ask for it. I forbid you from now on to sign the smallest act without my permission, even be it a mere passport. You shall inform me of everything day by day and favour no one". To suppose that such a peremptory and clearly formulated decision was taken *à l'instant* does not make sense. More simply, the day had come which, as the King himself dictated in his memoirs, *"Je souhaitais et craignais tout ensemble . . . depuis longtemps"*.

Blaise Pascal (1623–1662), in a portrait by Philippe de Champaigne. Born in the provinces at Clermand-Ferrand, he moved to Paris in 1647 to dedicate himself to study and research in physics and mathematics. At the end of 1654, the great French scientist and philosopher retired to the Abbey of Port-Royal to devote himself to the ascetic life. A few years later, he published eighteen *Lettres provinciales*, in defence of Jansenist ideas, which were condemned by the Sorbonne.

The Building of Grandeur

The First Hammer-Blows against Privileges

Louis XIV inherited a France at peace, reinforced within her borders with an international prestige which put her at the head of the European nations. The century-long struggle against the Habsburgs of Spain and Austria had been decisively resolved to the advantage of France. But, on the internal side many things did not work properly. The evil of the buying and selling of offices had resulted in an enormous bureaucracy, which bled only the productive classes, particularly the small farming landowners. The contract for tax-farming, which was allowed to private citizens, permitted incredible abuses: for example, the tax-farmers would advance to the State the total tax due and then generously recover their losses from the taxpayers. Embezzlements and illicit appropriations were part of everyday administration. Louis XIV went to work energetically.

From the very beginning of his reign, he arranged his time meticulously; on Mondays and Fridays he held the meetings of the State Council, where problems of general importance were treated; Tuesdays, Thursdays and Saturdays were dedicated to meetings of a financial character; on Thursday afternoons, the King, surrounded by the *Conseil de Conscience,* made up of his personal confessor and three prelates, allotted the benefices which had become vacant. He kept Wednesdays and Sundays for himself. Punctually every evening, as announced, he summoned his ministers, checked on their work and signed the acts.

He kept this rhythm of work almost unaltered to his very last days, with the exception of very brief periods of illness and travels within his country and to the battlefront. His personal energy and the dynamism which he infused into the work of his great collaborators, and which these in turn injected into the country, was the rightful boast of Louis XIV. But can one say that from the beginning he was motivated by a precise political plan?

It is easy to see how Louis's policies from the very first years were in direct continuity with those of Mazarin and of Richelieu, and even those of Sully and Henri IV. Faced both by a State structure and by a society which, in many respects, were falling apart, he had to make precise and immediate choices.

Though he did not wholly disregard the methods of his teacher, he nevertheless preferred Richelieu's technique of hammer-blows, which he found more suited to his character. For his own part, he added an irrepressible desire to assert himself (revenge, perhaps?) and to acquire *la gloire.* All historians seem to agree that he was no genius. Sainte-Beuve was probably right when he maintained that he "did not possess anything but commonsense, but a considerable dose of it", and "commonsense" suggested to him that a serious reform of the State must begin from the top.

His speech to the ministers on the day after Mazarin's death was not taken very seriously. Everybody was occupied in making predictions about who would be first minister. The idea that the King might take upon himself the charge of the government of the State was unthinkable. The image of the *roi fainéant,* the lazy king, suited only to feasts, ceremonies and frivolities was completely taken for granted. After all, Louis XIII had been in that mould. But with his son the memory of the Fronde and its lessons was very much alive. The King understood that his present and future credibility rested on his ability to govern and, therefore, he was totally committed to it. He created a *Conseil d'Etat* made up of only three ministers: Lionne, for diplomatic affairs; Le Tellier, the elder, for war and Fouquet, for finances.

The last-named deserves a few words. Nicolas Fouquet (1615–1680), son of a Breton shipowner recently ennobled, was the least malleable of the three, as he enjoyed an enormous fortune of his own and a strong network of connections. He was undoubtedly the favourite in the competition for the office of first minister. Like the other two, as a creature of Mazarin, he is a perfect example of a social climber of the time – ambitious, astute and amoral. His lack of prejudice made him an ideal collaborator for Mazarin, who had prized him more and more and eventually had nominated

Triumph of Louis XIV,
miniature by Joseph
Werner, German school of
the seventeenth century.

him Superintendent of Finances and Minister of State.

Profiting from his offices of State, he accumulated enormous wealth for the Cardinal as well as for himself which, in contrast to his teacher, he was happy to dissipate in extravagant luxuries and fabulous feasts. Just one ball cost him ten thousand gold *thalers,* and one dinner twelve thousand. But he also invested in lands and castles, in which he became a forerunner of the Louis XIV style by creating grandiose gardens and parks, with statues, fountains and marvellous artifices of water.

In pomp and patronage he was certainly a model for the Sun King. Lover of *belles-lettres* Fouquet encouraged the old Corneille to write *Oedipe,* was a friend of Madame de Scudéry and Pellisson, and his greatest merit was to protect Molière and La Fontaine at the beginning of their careers.

No wonder, then, that such a character should represent the greatest obstacle to the King's plans, especially since Fouquet himself in his boundless ambition set few limits on his career. In the first place he wanted to dominate the young monarch and take over his affairs and then use him as a further instrument of power and prestige. Part of the plan was to push the King into dissipations and pleasures which would undermine his public image.

To this end, he could count on numerous faithful associates, whom he had at Court and who occupied the main public offices. He was generous in personal gifts to the King and he even went so far as trying to corrupt the Queen Mother. However, he knew very well that the most powerful weapon in his intrigues was *la femme.* He used a personal, intimate acquaintance who had been the "first love" of the King, Olympe Mancini, Comtesse de Soissons, who became the first in the long series of the King's extra-marital adventures. However, Fouquet had not taken into account the fact that the King had now been "initiated" and that he had learned, as he was able to write in his memoirs, to keep the affairs of the heart separate from those of the State.

Furthermore, there was another character who had his own designs: Jean-Baptiste Colbert. The latter, already an ex-associate of Mazarin and administrator of his wealth, kept the King constantly informed of the acts and intentions of

View and perspective of Vaux-le-Vicomte from the gardens, engraving by Israel Silvestre. More than a *chateau,* Nicolas Fouquet's residence was a veritable palace.

Fouquet, who was his superior. Having quickly abandoned his first love, the King was soon attracted by the graces of Louise de La Vallière, and thus extracted himself from the machinations of his minister. (Fouquet tried to bribe this last mistress too, but unsuccessfully). Pretending to be unaware of the plots, Louis kept Fouquet as a minister and treated him with the usual respect, but in reality he was only waiting for the right moment to strike. The teachings of Mazarin were starting to bear their fruit. At first, the King induced Fouquet to sell his office of General Procurator as unworthy of his person, in order to be able to deprive him of the right of being judged by Parliament. For the same reason, he nominated Colbert in his place as Superintendent of Finances. The latter was therefore easily able to provide the King with proof of the frauds perpetrated by his predecessor.

Obviously Fouquet suspected something, particularly since as a precaution he had begun to fortify his castles, but his high opinion of himself and the affability shown by the King were so great that he was deceived. Louis took him by surprise after a grand feast given by Fouquet at the castle of Vaux-le-Vicomte on 17th August, 1661, in honour of the King and the Court. If the King had had any doubts about the frauds of his minister, these would have been dismissed by the splendour of that residence (the work of Le Vau and Le Nôtre), the thirty-six dozen heavy gold plates and the five hundred silver plates displayed during a dinner which had cost twenty thousand *livres*. The trap closed shortly afterwards when Fouquet was on his way towards his domain of Belle-Île in Brittany. The powerful minister was arrested during the journey by a musketeer called d'Artagnan. In accordance with the plan, Fouquet's castles were immediately besieged and conquered by the King's troops.

This event is very revealing. In particular, it allows one to understand the real relations of power inside France, if the King himself, in order to affirm his own authority, had to have recourse to such expedients. This authority was very weak for some time to come, as is shown by the fact that the tribunal charged with judging Fouquet was set up with difficulty three full years later and in the end, on 14th November, 1664, condemned him to the mild penalty of exile. But the King, *motu proprio,* had him locked up for life in the

In this portrait, Jean-Baptiste Colbert displays the satisfied expression of a successful man, which is amply justified by the role he played in conducting French affairs; he was almost another Richelieu or Mazarin, with particular expertise in the field of finance and commerce.

strong fortress of Pignerol, where he died in 1680. It is appropriate at this point to mention the famous "velvet mask", which Voltaire and the elder Dumas subsequently turned into an "iron mask". Both writers had Fouquet in mind. The character in the "velvet mask" (a prisoner disguised to conceal the terrible disfigurement of his face or really to hide his identity), is undoubtedly historical. The most likely candidate for this role, however, seems to be the Piedmontese diplomat, Mattioli, who played a double game with France and Spain during the negotiations over Casale-Monferrato.

The King had achieved several objectives through the Fouquet affair: he had rid himself of a dangerous enemy, he had given a demonstration of his own energy and intentions and he had acquired a precious associate in the person of Jean-Baptiste Colbert.

Colbert and the Financial Reform

Colbert was born at Rheims in 1619, the son of a wool merchant. His father made him study in Paris, with the intention of setting him on a career of "offices", which would lead to the attainment of the aristocratic title *de robe* – a typical ambition for the middle classes of the time. Having entered the Ministry of War at a very early age by virtue of his undoubted capacities, Colbert shortly became secretary to the minister, Michel Le Tellier.

The omnipotent Mazarin, who had an infallible flair for discerning the abilities of young bureaucrats, very soon noticed him: in 1649 he nominated him Councillor of the State and, from 1651 onwards, wished him at his own side and held him in such great esteem that in 1656 he entrusted him with the administration of his own possessions. On Mazarin's death he revealed to the King the secret places where the Cardinal had hidden considerable amounts of money (according to rumours these amounted to fifteen million gold *scudi*). The King expressed his gratitude by elevating him within a few years to the highest offices: in 1664 he named him Superintendent of the Fleet, in 1665 he also conferred on him the office of General Controller of Finances, in 1668 that of Secretary of State for the Royal Household, and the following year Secretary for the Navy. Having become Marquis de Seignelay and Marquis de Chateauneuf, he accumulated power and influence over the King, such as no one else was able to do.

"Colbertism" (the term used for the first time by the Italian economist, Francesco Mengotti, in a work of 1797, which bore this title) was not a true economic doctrine, but rather a practice dominated by the idea of "rationalising" the processes of production and distribution of goods and thereby gearing the whole process to the financial interests of the State.

Moreover, Colbert did not introduce substantial reforms, but only corrections, which had the object of limiting the most apparent abuses and malfunctions. In view of the gravity and urgency of the financial situation, the first measure was to set up a tribunal, ordered by the King to use the maximum severity. Its function was to prevent illegal appropriations by financial officers and, as

a result of its work, many tax-farmers and employees of the treasury were hit by such heavy fines that they were reduced to ruin, whilst guilty officials of lower status were condemned to death. During the two years, 1662 and 1663, seventy million *livres* were recovered by the public treasury, the equivalent of half the entire budget. More articulate and incisive measures were to follow. The original determining idea, very simple and praiseworthy in itself, was to lessen the tax-load on productive activities and to hit unproductive incomes. The size of the *taille* was greatly reduced, a tax which was a veritable scourge for the lower classes. At the same time, all the noble titles granted during the past thirty years, and the tax exemption they entailed, were abolished. With an arbitrary decision, the public debt of the State was abruptly reduced: part of the incomes from it were bought back by the State at the original price (the *rentiers* were used to selling their entitlements at an increased price); amid much dissatisfaction and agitation, all incomes from the State had their rate of interest reduced by one fifth.

The decision taken in 1664 to abolish the internal customs duties between the provinces of the

Michel Le Tellier, Lord of Chaville, in a portrait by a painter of the contemporary French school. From 1643 onwards, he was Secretary of State for War and in 1677 he was appointed Chancellor. Historians accord great importance to his military work.

During the seventeenth century, the Gobelins factory produced a series of tapestries to commemorate great events in the life of Louis XIV. The series was designed by Charles Le Brun assisted among others by his nephew, Adam Frans Van der Meulen and H. Testelin. In the tapestry reproduced here, the King accompanied by Colbert is shown visiting the factory.

north and those of the south, and to limit customs duty collection to the country's borders, was particularly important for the development of commerce and of the economy in general.

"Colbertism" was, as is well known, a heavy form of protectionism and within a brief period it attained some noteworthy advantages: it protected the internal market from foreign competition, particularly Dutch, which remained a constant obsession with Colbert to the point of inducing him to encourage the war against the Netherlands, it favoured the birth of new industries and it allowed the Ministry of Finances to control the flow of money and goods, in modern terms the "balance of payments", with sufficient precision. Already at this time the order of the day was to reduce imports and increase exports. To achieve this final goal, Colbert employed measures of a typically interventionist character. All types of industry were rigidly organised in corporations; even the quality and specifications of products were laid down by means of regulations and transgressing these regulations involved heavy sanctions. The State itself became an entrepreneur: the manufacture of Gobelins tapestries and that of Saint-Gobain glass became Royal property and the King lent money and became involved in many other industries.

A large operation of "Frenchification" of all that was best in Europe in terms of commercial products was mounted. Masters and craftsmen from all countries were attracted to France, with the prospect of large earnings: Murano glassblowers to Saint-Gobain, Lombard silk-makers to Lyons, Dutch weavers to Abbeville, English wool-makers and potters: industry flourished everywhere. In the meantime, Colbert gave a boost to the merchant navy by creating shipping companies on the English and Dutch model.

A considerable commercial improvement characterised the first years. French goods, and luxury goods in particular (lace of different kinds, brocades, tapestries, faience, glass, and so on) began to conquer the most important European markets. So began the process of French "colonisation" of Europe in terms of taste and fashion, which would last well beyond the reign of Louis XIV. But the negative effects of the policies soon became apparent. Gradually all the other countries increased their customs duties to such an extent that they paralysed or entirely blocked complete areas of trade. Thus, war was inevitable.

The Power of the King

While the reorganisation of finance was thought out and conducted by Colbert, Louis concentrated on building up his own authority and began by punishing the old protagonists of the Fronde and first among them Parliament.

In December, 1661, he had all the public acts which had been approved during the period of the revolt delivered to him and publicly tore them up with his own hands. Many members were dismissed following the decree, which abolished all the titles of the nobility acquired during the last thirty years, a decree which had been devised specifically to punish Parliament. The official title of this body was degraded from "sovereign court" to "supreme court". The story goes that, coming back one afternoon from hunting, the King came to the assembly in his sporting clothes (which for the times was a considerable insult) and, riding whip in hand, threatened Parliament with disciplinary measures because of slight delays in the registration of acts. In just a few years, Parliament had its functions reduced to protocol only.

In waging his personal war against the "old powers", the King's autocratic style of government resulted in the long term in the creation of a powerful, centralised state bureaucracy. Royal ordinances were applied in the provinces by "intendants" of bourgeois extraction, who not being titled office-holders could be dismissed at any moment and therefore had an interest in exercising their function loyally. The importance of these functionaries grew to such an extent that, as the future "prefects" of the State, they became the veritable backbone of its administration. They were the means by which the King suppressed abuses and repressed the nobles and high prelates. This institution answered perfectly to the plan of limiting all forms of local autonomy, which had given so much trouble to Richelieu and Mazarin. The provinces were placed under the authority of governors, usually nobles appointed for life, assisted by local parliaments charged with administrative and judicial functions. Louis abruptly reduced the governors' period of office to three years, and gave the intendants powers of control over the acts of the parliaments and the "municipalities". Only a few *pays d'etats,* such as Brittany and Languedoc (that is to say, the provinces governed by assemblies uniting nobility, clergy and the Third Estate), kept certain forms of autonomy for a time. These included the right to fix the total amount of taxes and the ways in which they were applied to the inhabitants and to decide by vote the extent of the *don gratuit* to the King. This situation did not last long, however. In little more than ten years, all the regional institutions which might possibly interfere with the King's powers (parliaments, governors, provincial estates and municipalities) were gradually deprived of all real power. Louis abolished the use of "books of grievances" and decided to fix the amount of the *don gratuit* himself. His old rancour against "separate bodies", instigators of Frondes, was probably the main inspiration of his great reform of the State.

The nobles did not fare much better. Kept away from public offices, they got their own back with the connivance of the judges by increasing the feudal burdens of the peasants. This happened particularly in the provinces. The King set up commissions, which were a type of tribunal with wide powers and sent them to the provinces, where they held extraordinary sessions given the significant name of "great days".

In 1665, in Auvergne and neighbouring provinces, three-hundred-and-forty-nine nobles were forced to run away to escape the death penalty, ninety-six were sent into exile and the greater part of their belongings was confiscated. It should be noted, however, that they belonged to a nobility which was "of the blood", but minor and their possessions were largely in a decayed state and they were therefore particularly greedy. But justice so severely applied by magistrates of bourgeois origins, while producing the predictable popular enthusiasm, also had the effect of intimidating the greater nobility who, having seen the way the wind was blowing, began to behave with that adulation and servility which characterised their attitude towards the King during the years of the full splendour of Louis XIV.

On the other hand, the King systematically started to use the high nobility as his diplomats and representatives. This responsibility was entrusted to another valued associate. Hugues de Lionne (1611–1671), but the King also kept a close watch on it and held it under strict and continuous control. The King realised from the beginning the importance of diplomacy for the grandeur and image of personal *gloire* which he wished to foster.

H. Testelin, *Louis XIV, patron of the Royal Academy of Painting and Sculpture*. This painting, like many others, illustrates the personal "grandeur" that the Sun King wanted and was able to build up.

31

The Diplomacy of the Sun King

For a long time attempts had been made to establish the theoretical foundations of international law. Nevertheless, problems of relations between powers were in actual fact resolved either by tradition or quite often by unilateral decision. Only the Most Serene Republic of Venice maintained permanent diplomatic delegations in all the capitals of Europe, as it had done since the beginning of the sixteenth century; the Holy Church of Rome also had its apostolic nuncios, but these were often purely local prelates. International law, the offspring of empirical practice, had in fact some strange aspects. For example, there existed a right of *transitus innoxius* across non-belligerent countries which found themselves caught between two other countries which were at war (the army had to pass through by stages, respect people and property and reimburse any damage caused).

The *droit de cloche* allowed admirals to remove the bells of maritime towns which they had taken or to exact a heavy ransom in compensation. The question of maritime safety was always a thorny problem. When two ships of different nationality crossed at sea, the normal usage was that they should salute each other by firing a cannon and lowering the flag. This worked very well until arguments of power and prestige intervened, then there were sensational incidents with cannonades and sinkings. The English, with the Treaty of Westminster (1654), confirmed later at Breda in 1667, imposed on the Dutch the obligation to salute first. With the French, the problem was not easily resolved. Richelieu had tried to conclude an agreement, which remained a dead letter, on the problem that both sides were held to be equal.

From 1661, Louis XIV contested a usage, established for a long time at the initiative of Mazarin, according to which the English had priority in the North Sea and the French in the Atlantic. Negotiations were begun, without success, after which English and French ships avoided meeting each other for a long time, although they were allies.

Claude-Guy Halle, *Reparation made by the Duke of Genoa to Louis XIV*. The naval salute, which the French King exacted for his own fleet, cost the Genoese republic enormous damage and humiliation.

However, the King was completely intractable towards the Spanish, the Dutch and the Genoese on this point. At the beginning, the French merchant and naval fleet found itself in a situation of numerical inferiority: hardly five or six hundred out of some twenty-thousand ships, which ploughed the seas at this period were French and she had only twenty warships in all. In a few years, Colbert as Superintendent of the Fleet and then Minister of the Marine carried the number of warships up to three hundred and merchant shipping to more than two thousand. This allowed the French to provoke serious incidents, purely out of motives of etiquette. In 1679, Louis expressly ordered his admirals to attack Spanish galleys which had not been the first to salute. In 1685, although the two nations were not at war, Admiral de Tourville gave battle to the Spanish fleet in front of Alicante, for not having received the priority of homage which was his "due". In the course of the following years, the same thing happened twice to the Dutch fleet.

It was worse for the Genoese. In 1678, a French squadron was sent in front of the Ligurian port to demand the right of salute; when it was refused, it was bombarded by more than a thousand cannon shots. The bombardment suffered by the town in 1684 was much more terrible, but at least it was justified by a specific plan to conquer the town, although this was small consolation.

Significantly, only the Turks were treated with any regard, because Louis relied on their expansion towards the Balkans and towards central Europe to weaken the Habsburg Empire. In 1668, when his Ambassador sailed for Constantinople, the King ordered him not to display the French flag, in order to avoid complications on the question of saluting it. However, he retaliated with the Barbary states of the African coast, possibly because he believed them to be independent from the Sacred Porte. In 1681, with the Treaty of Algiers, he demanded that every time a ship of the "Emperor of France" (which was the title Louis liked to use with these people) put down its anchor in front of the Algerian port, all the ships present should salute it with numerous cannon shots. It was only after the Peace of Ryswick in 1697, that Louis became more tolerant towards the ships of republics.

The diplomatic arrogance of the Most Christian King did not even given way before the leader of the whole of Christendom. By skilfully provoking incidents at Rome between the Pope's Corsican guards and the guards of the French Ambassador, the Duc de Créqui, Louis seized the opportunity to invade Avignon in 1662 and to threaten the Papal state with war. From then on, the Corsicans had to give up the much coveted honour of serving the Pope.

We have mentioned a few of the most striking examples to give an idea of the conditions of international law and of the "bite" which Louis gave to his diplomacy. It is not possible to say that he shone on account of his "fair play" because he rarely kept his agreements, nor his *esprit de finesse*. Essentially, he used two tools: intimidation, as we have seen, and money which he distributed in enormous sums, driving Colbert to despair, to corrupt.

Charles II and James II of England, who in money matters had their hands tied by Parliament, were for a long time subsidised by Louis. In addition he bribed English and Dutch parliamentarians and ministers and financed the Great Elector of Brandenburg and other German princes in order to disengage them from the influence of the Empire. In 1662 he bought back Dunkirk from England for four million *livres,* an amount which he predictably did not then pay in full. Furthermore, as a reward for his support, which partly went against his own national interests, he granted Charles II a pension for life (a rather curious gift for a King to make).

The only pleasing aspect of his diplomacy, for which as we have said foreigners were to be grateful to him, was that of sending the great nobles of France who were, in fact, often weak and incompetent, abroad as diplomats and plenipotentiaries to teach a bit of *savoir-faire* to the rough provincials.

Begun by Mathieu and completed by Pierre Sève, the tapestry of which this is a detail, represents Louis XIV with his *bâton du commandement* in his hand. He is about to make his entry into the town of Dunkirk, one of his first territorial acquisitions.

The Great War Machine

The army too needed to be reorganised, since it was as antiquated and inefficient as the rest of the administration. The officer ranks from captain upwards, with the exception of Marshal of France and *generalissimo,* were for sale, as were the commandership-in-chief of particular corps. When an army was being recruited, the high commissioners passed on this duty to a certain number of colonels or captains, who would directly recruit, clothe and arm the troops, taking from the State one allowance per man.

This turned the army into a kind of hierarchy of fiefs, took away any effective power from the State and encouraged all manner of abuse. Colonels and captains, who were responsible for the administration of regiments and companies, made their lists seem much larger than they really were. In the event of parades or inspections, they hurriedly dressed up servants, vagrants and all sorts of "extras". The discipline and fighting spirit were on a par with the organisation.

Louis, with the help of the two Le Telliers, put some order into this sector. Michel Le Tellier, Seigneur of Chaville (1603–1685) and from 1669 on, François-Michel, his son, Marquis de Louvois (1641–1691), were the main instigators and executors of this reform. Michel, of bourgeois origin, had been trained, as might be expected, in Mazarin's shadow, but he had little in common with the Cardinal's personality besides sagacity and administrative shrewdness. A mild and withdrawn character, he compensated for his lack of inspiration by hard work. His son was much more like Mazarin and the Cardinal placed him at an extremely young age at the Ministry of War and entrusted important duties to him. But the wisdom and moderation of Michel Le Tellier was not inherited by his son who was pitiless, cynical and a bully. He also committed a number of crimes that went unpunished. In his favour, however, he had a notable administrative capacity, a sense of realism, versatility and great perseverance in bringing projects to completion.

As with the economy, attempts were made in the first instance to correct the most obvious defects. With the new ruling of 1661, extremely harsh and degrading punishments were threatened for frauds concerning the size of lists of soldiers and inspectors were appointed, directly dependent on

ESERCITO DI S.M. LUIGI XIV RE DI FRANCIA
1706

The build-up of the great army of Louis XIV, which for a long time numbered two hundred thousand men, took place gradually. Many modifications were dictated by the experience of war. In this print we see a sergeant of the grenadiers of the regiment *Dauphin* and a fusillier of the regiment *Tournaisis.*

the minister and with wide disciplinary powers. The office of commander-in-chief could no longer be bought, but only conferred by the King.

The manner in which soldiers should be armed was minutely prescribed; about a third of the French infantry were still armed with antiquated weapons such as pikes; from 1679 onwards, however, Louis eliminated them almost completely and in their place introduced the bayonet inserted on the barrel of the musket.

The build-up of Louis's great army, which for a long time numbered two-hundred-thousand men, took place gradually and many modifications were dictated by war experience. It became progressively more difficult to purchase the lower officer ranks and new intermediate ranks were introduced to fill the gaps between the marshal commanding thirty-thousand men and the colonel with only four-hundred men.

The real innovation was, however, the introduction of special "corps" with well-defined duties: regiments of artillery, grenadiers, dragoons, corps of sappers and experts in placing mines.

Finally, the uniform was introduced to avoid confusion in battle, but above all to avoid desertions, which were all too frequent.

The first six years of Louis's reign were relatively peaceful and as we have seen were devoted to reorganising the State. The guiding idea of this operation was admirably straightforward. It moved on three planes represented by the three sole ministers, instead of the previous twenty-four, who made up the *Conseil d'État* (Finance, Diplomacy and War). They had one objective: to make France a power unrivalled in Europe. If the plan was in itself extremely clear, the choice of "enemies" was often instinctive and impulsive. Louis held for a long time that the main obstacle to the greatness of France was still Spain, a country undergoing a process of decline and decay – though it was perhaps the knowledge of its very vulnerability which aroused his greed.

As Mazarin had foreseen, Spain found herself able to pay only a small part of the enormous sum promised as a dowry for Marie-Thérèse in exchange for renouncing rights of succession to the throne. The French King did not insist too much on the payment and applied pressure only in order to exact the official recognition of his wife's rights. He even went so far as to promise to Spain the Duchy of Luxembourg, the French Hainault and Cambrai.

Philip IV remained immovable and at his death in 1665 he left a will, which formally excluded the House of Bourbon from the succession to Spain. Louis, then, had to look for other pretexts and he set his jurists to work. The desire to endow all his disputes with a legal respectability was a constant factor in Louis's policies.

There was a particular custom in Brabant pertaining to civil law, whereby the inheritance of a fief went to the children of the first marriage and had to be "devolved" on them at the death of the father, while any children by a second marriage were entirely excluded. This custom seemed to fit the case of Philip IV precisely who, having re-married in 1649 left his throne to the little Charles II, the child of the second marriage and, to Louis's great disappointment, born the same year as the Dauphin of France (1661).

It is irrelevant to say that this attempt to succeed to the throne had no justified foundation. Louis himself was well aware of this, so much so that he insisted that the Regent Maria-Anna of Austria should declare her acceptance of the right of "devolution" at least for Flanders. Her denial was, however, absolute. The Habsburgs were his *bêtes noires* and his "sacred rights" having been abused, the King decided to uphold them through war.

In the Spring of 1667, the French troops, under

the command of Turenne, entered Belgian Flanders. They found little resistance and spent some time besieging strongholds which fell into their hands without bringing them any particular glory. Louis felt the need to reaffirm his right to "devolution" by means of an official document in which he also invoked moral principle, condemning the "intemperance of a second marriage", although he himself had already fathered several bastards. The immediate effect of entering war, however, was that of bringing about the Peace of Breda in July, 1667, between England and Holland, who had been fighting each other since 1665. Furthermore, these two countries and Sweden, contracted an alliance against France.

At this point, Louis decided to give a more decisive turn to the war: at the end of February, 1668, French troops under the Prince de Condé, who had been pardoned for the occasion, invaded Franche-Comté and overran it within a fortnight. War flared up again in Flanders, where other strongholds capitulated within a short time. The Spanish governor of the Netherlands, the Marquis of Castel-Rodrigo, valiant but hopelessly outnumbered, was forced to save what he could by starting peace negotiations. Peace was completed at Aix-la-Chapelle on 2nd May, 1668. Spain recovered Franche-Comté, but gave up most of the towns which had fallen into French hands: Charleroi, Tournai, Lille, Coutrai and Bergues. During the years which run from the Peace of Aix-la-Chapelle to the beginning of the war with the Netherlands, efforts were concentrated on

Philip VI, painted here in an equestrian portrait by Velasquez, was an indolent Sovereign of weak character. Like his father, he was at the mercy of favourites such as the Duke of Olivares and from 1643, Luis de Haro. He was not able to avoid either the Court intrigues or the military defeats which determined the crumbling of Spanish power.

further improving the army and on siege techniques. The King was following the plans and preparations with a real "sporting" passion. Meanwhile, his minister Louvois found a valuable associate in the person of Sébastien Le Prestre de Vauban (1633–1707). Of the great figures that surrounded Louis, he was possibly the most upright and least servile. A first-rank military technician, he surrounded France with a belt of strongholds which held out for some centuries.

Louis decided to attack the Dutch "barrier forts". Colbert was certainly the originator of this idea. These "carriers of the seas", with their twelve thousand merchantmen, were an obsession with him. His commercial doctrine, conceived as a customs war, collided with the vitality of Dutch trade, which he had always envied and sought to imitate. This time the King had no legal pretext. He was even bound to Holland by a treaty of alliance and to Jan De Witt by a personal friendship. To prepare the ground he had recourse, in the grand style, to diplomacy by corruption (costing some several million *livres*), directed towards Charles II of England, through the intermediary of his sister Henrietta, Duchesse d'Orléans. By the sudden invasion of Lorraine, he intimidated the German states and even the Emperor, the feeble Leopold, who in 1671 signed a treaty of non-intervention. The treaty was the last work of Lionne, who died the same year.

Having concluded a treaty of friendship with Sweden in April 1672, everything was ready for the war. Charles II invented pretexts and provoked incidents; Louis XIV did not even attempt to look for excuses, and declared war on Holland on 1st April 1672. France put one hundred-and-eighty thousand men into the field and could count on the naval support of England. The King and his Court were euphoric, foreseeing a success similar to the War of Devolution. The first actions were conclusive.

Instead of attacking the "barrier forts" on the Flemish side in the first assault, the French army invaded the Dutch territory directly, passing along an arm of the Rhine, the Lek. This became, in the exalted talk of the courtiers, the "passage of the Rhine". At the end of June, out of the seven united provinces, only Holland itself and Zealand remained free.

Louis XIV had expressly ordered the army to "devour the country"; the troops obeyed. The

spoiling, sacking, burning and threats resulted not in intimidating the people, but in the exact opposite: they were determined to fight to their last breath. The great Admiral de Ruyter checked the Anglo-French fleet in the Bay of Soule, and defended the coast with great determination. Louis was looking forward to victory and answered requests for peace with totally unacceptable demands. Jan and Cornelius De Witt, responsible for the negotiations were lynched by the people of Amsterdam, who acclaimed the twenty-one-year-old William of Orange-Nassau, as war commander.

The Dutch broke down the great sea-dams thereby isolating a large part of the territory, which dashed the King's hopes for a quick triumph. He had followed his army in person and had crossed the "Rhine", but he was forced to return to Paris in a hurry in order to control the international situation more effectively.

Meanwhile, Spain had entered the war, the Empire had sent an army led by old Montecuccoli to the upper Rhine, and also Frederick William, Elector of Brandenburg, had intervened with a special expeditionary force. Having set out

Sébastien Le Prestre, Lord of Vauban, successfully tested the siege techniques he had devised in person on more than fifty occasions. This diagram on the uses of an attacking position is taken from his work, *The Way in which to attack Positions.*

Joseph Parrocel, *The Passage of the Rhine*. Little more than a century later, Napoleon Bonaparte defined a feat of arms as an "operation of the fourth rank".

to "devour" the Netherlands, Louis was now faced by a strong coalition, partly due to the diplomacy of the House of Orange, but the main factor was the final realisation by the Habsburgs that, had the Netherlands fallen, Louis would have been unstoppable.

France was forced to divert her forces against her new enemies, which gave the Dutch some respite. Vauban provided a model of his military art in 1673 at the seige of Maestricht, the last Dutch stronghold on the Maas, but during the same year Admiral de Ruýter defeated the Anglo-French fleet on three consecutive occasions. Two happenings favourable to the Dutch marked the year 1674; the entry into the war of the Danes, on their side; and the retreat of England, imposed on Charles II by the anger of the people who were irritated by numerous defeats. The Emperor succeeded in persuading most of the German princes to leave the French orbit and they united against Louis.

France was left alone, but her armies demonstrated that technically they were distinctly superior to the "old school" armies of the allies. Vauban invaded Franche-Comté and conquered it in a few weeks; Turenne beat the Imperial troops several times (after Montecuccoli had retired, following disagreements); and the Grand Condé beat William of Orange himself at Seneffe on 11th August, 1674. But they were not decisive victories, because in that period the slow pace at which wars were conducted allowed the defeated to regroup. The spring of 1675 saw the French take the offensive, they always did at the beginning of their campaigns. Turenne occupied new strongholds in Flanders, which opened the road to Holland for him. However, on 27th July, as he found himself faced by the army of Raimondo Montecuccoli, who had allowed himself to be persuaded into resuming the command. In the course of this battle at Sassbach, Turenne died after being hit by a cannonball. The French army had to retreat and Montecuccoli took advantage from this to invade Alsace.

1676 also saw the French armies take the offensive. Louis, convinced that he would be able to deliver a decisive attack, put himself at the head of the army in Flanders, assisted by Vauban. Near Maestricht, which was besieged by William, he went within cannon range of the enemy lines, although Louvois made sure he would be sufficiently protected. He realised perhaps that he could take the place of a good general and, being angry with Louvois, he conclusively retired from the battlefield taking Vauban with him.

William of Orange was afterwards forced to retreat and during that year, the Netherlands suffered yet another very serious loss with the death of Admiral de Ruyter, which took place during a naval engagement near Catania (22nd April, 1676). The year 1677 began on an even worse note for the Dutch. François-Henri de Montmorency-Bouteville, Duc de Luxembourg (1628–1695), had a particular liking for out-of-season campaigns. In the middle of March, in very intense cold, he began to lay siege to Valenciennes and Saint-Omer. William had hurriedly to collect a great army and mount a rescue attempt. At Cassel on 11th April he sustained a heavy defeat: he lost many men and all the artillery at his disposal.

Having been defeated several times in war, William was none-the-less firmly determined "to win the peace". Charles II of England, despite being indebted to Louis by many promises and millions of *livres,* was being pushed by public opinion into war with France, which put him in a very difficult position. To keep public opinion at bay, he was forced to put pressure on both sides to arrive at a solution to the conflict as soon as possible. He invited William III to England, who arrived there in October 1677. The two discussed not only the peace, but also a problem of capital importance for the history of Europe.

Charles II did not have any direct heirs. The succession would go to his brother, James of York, who only had two daughters, Mary and Anne. The problem was to resist the pressure of Louis, who was asking too insistently for the hand of Mary for the Dauphin. He was willing to renounce the dowry and offered a great amount of money. His pressing insistence was, with just reason, considered suspect and dangerous for the future of England. A marriage to William seemed the best solution and it offered the advantage of facing Louis with a *fait accompli* during eventual peace negotiations. The official betrothal took place on 31st October and the marriage was celebrated on 14th November.

The insult mortally wounded Louis's pride, but curiously turned out to be a factor in bringing about the peace. In his own way, Louis always remained a legalist, so that, when his direct plan failed, he cultivated the idea of attracting Orange into his own orbit. Charles II offered himself as a peace mediator, but the first proposals which gave little reward to France, who was the victor on the battlefield, were rejected by Louis with disdain. Indeed, they were turned down with an intensification of the war.

Saint-Ghislain had fallen in December and in the Spring of 1678 the French offensive seemed to sweep away all the Dutch defences. Louvois gave a proof of his ability by taking Ghent, the most populous city of Flanders after Brussels, in just eight days. The latter was defended with difficulty by Orange. Meanwhile, the news of the French victories mobilised the whole of England. Charles found himself unable to procrastinate any longer and had to prepare an expeditionary force.

At Nijmegen the peace negotiations had been open a long time. Louis was uncharacteristically generous, perhaps due to the threat of the English intervention or perhaps to some inner conviction that the war operations were going to be protracted. To avoid lengthy negotiations, on 1st April he sent an ultimatum postponed in the end to August, with which he satisfied the most important Dutch requests, namely the abolition of customs duties and a preferential commercial treaty. Having got these concessions the Dutch "merchants" hurriedly concluded the Peace of Nijmegen on 10th August, 1678, without William's knowledge, whilst he was near Mons attacking the Duc de Luxembourg.

William, beside himself after the "sell-out" of the peace, none-the-less had to give in. In fact, however, in spite of the loss of some "barrier forts", Holland emerged from the war keeping its national integrity and with a precious commercial treaty which represented a true defeat for Colbert and his economic policy.

Various peace treaties were being signed right up until June, 1679: with Spain, Denmark, Sweden and the Empire. These different treaties were unilateral *diktats* of Louis, who derived prestige and respect from them. His territorial gains, however, although considerable, were not proportionate to the effort and riches expended. In the final analysis, the Sovereign had failed to achieve his initial objective: to "devour" the republic of the seven United Provinces.

The Sun King and his Court

During the period which ran from the Peace of Nijmegen to the death of Colbert, Louis XIV perfected the image of the Sun King, both in the eyes of the Court and of foreigners.

It is not easy for history to recreate the personality of Louis XIV in a single image and it would perhaps be more accurate to leave him with his contradictions. It is difficult to reconcile the meticulous and fussy activity with the amorous dissipation, the "divine" bearing with the constant distrust, the licentiousness with the bigotry. There is, however, no conflicting image to set against the disproportionate self-love which prevented Louis from having the slightest vestige of self-doubt. In his memoirs there is no trace of true remorse. He often retained mediocre associates, solely because to change them would have been a sign of fallibility. In his writings there is no trace of genuine remorse either, except, somewhat late in the day at the point of death, when he expressed his regret at "having loved glory too much". In his memoirs, justifying his refusal to treat with the Dutch, he writes, significantly, that posterity could if it so wished attribute this refusal to his ambition and to his desire to avenge himself for past insults, but he will not attempt to justify this ambition and desire. Ambition and love of glory are always excusable in a prince and particularly in a prince who was favoured by so much good fortune.

Although Louis professed to have an arrogant disdain for its judgement, his constant preoccupation with posterity is interesting. It is one of the surest clues to the interpretation of the *opération grandeur*. He had chosen for himself the sun emblem right from the first years of his reign, on the occasion of the festivities marking the baptism of the Dauphin (also called Louis, naturally), his

The work of an anonymous artist of the French school of the seventeenth century, this austere painting represents *Louis XIV at the Conseil des Parties*. The King was a true dictator and chose to intervene personally in all the affairs of the State. He increasingly came to identify his own person with the State.

only legitimate son, born to Marie-Thérèse on 1st November, 1661. The motto he adopted is also significant: *Nec pluribus impar*. It seemed to give a warning of the future development of great European conflicts. It is doubtful if he ever pronounced the concise formula, *L'Etat c'est moi:* all the same, it sums up the essence of his thought. He constantly reminded ministers and courtiers that the sole principle of the law was the will of the Sovereign, meaning his own, and he conducted himself accordingly.

It is hard to find in history a personality so completely egocentric. Although he had a fit and robust constitution, he was nevertheless preoccupied with his health, which must have been truly exceptional to resist the "cures" of the medicine of the time. In relationships with others he concentrated on emphasising the grandeur of his person. His comportment was always measured, almost affected, with a certain haughtiness that he may have taken from his mother. He was courteous to all the women he met, even servants.

When approaching forty (1675), as his hair began to recede, which was decidedly unworthy of a semi-divine being, he began to wear the curly wig with which the artists of the time immortalised him and which aroused the infatuation and admiration of all the courts of Europe. His cult of appearance was not only a means of "keeping his distance", but certainly also covered a profound insecurity: he was constantly suspicious, he read private correspondence, he surrounded himself with a host of informers and he was constantly within the sight of his Swiss guards.

Even his fear of being surpassed by his ministers must be considered from this viewpoint. In fact, he often let himself be led by Colbert and by Louvois, but one can imagine the thankless work it was for them making him believe it was always he alone who took the decisions. The King, afraid of their intelligence and their prestige, set them against each other, in order to preserve all the better his personal authority, even going so far as to make them unpopular.

All this only confirms the picture of a great psychological insecurity; but it did not only show itself in innate malignancy or political calculation. The flood of reverences and the adulation of the Court were such that it would have been necessary to have had a stomach like Pantagruel (or a greatly reduced intelligence) to have swallowed it without any other motive than personal vanity. In fact, on deeper analysis, one finds in the splendour and the emphasis on ceremonial, a subtle logic, in perfect accord with his political design of consolidating the monarchy.

Life at Court became an interminable theatrical performance. At banquets the dishes filed by in procession, served by eleven butlers. Lunch and breakfast followed rules of detailed ceremony.

When Louis XIV breakfasted, only the Queen was allowed to sit next to him: the others, including Monsieur Philippe, his brother, had to remain standing, ready to hand him whatever he needed. The Court at full strength had to be present at mass, which he himself never missed, even during his periods of great dissoluteness. The nobles used to turn their backs to the altar, their eyes fixed on the King installed in the gallery. From the ceremony of the *lever* to that of the

Pierre Mignard, *Marie-Thérèse, Queen of France and the Grand Dauphin.* The King wrote some *Memoires* for the education of his son, in which he condensed all his political wisdom and his personal conception of the tasks and duties of a prince.

41

coucher, the whole life of the Court revolved around its star.

Love affairs also enter into the picture. Except for numerous escapades with the Court ladies or with rich commoners occasionally favoured with the royal choice, three favourites mark the stages of the King's life: Louise de La Baume Le Blanc, Duchesse de La Vallière; Françoise-Athénaïs de Rochechouart, Marquise de Montespan and Françoise d'Aubigné, Marquise de Maintenon. After Olympe Mancini, the King was attracted by the fragile beauty of Louise de La Vallière, lady-in-waiting to his sister-in-law, Henrietta Stuart. Wagging tongues claimed that the King was taken with his brilliant English sister-in-law, and that Louise, who was slightly lame, was only a "screen". It is nevertheless certain that in spite of, or because of, her reserved character she was able to keep the heart of Louis XIV for several years.

Louise was barely sixteen and had received a deeply religious education. The sorrow that she felt for Marie-Thérèse and recurring remorse made her a difficult and temperamental mistress. Louis XIV, in contrast, already "toughened" as he always was in his emotional relationships, was unaware of the tears of his wife and of his ageing mother, who died precisely at this time in 1666. While following the army during the War of Devolution, her feelings of remorse grew more acute when she had to share the role of favourite with Montespan.

In 1671 she fled for the first time to a convent where, on the King's orders, Colbert went to bring her back. In 1674, with the King's consent, she entered the Carmelite convent permanently and died there in 1710. She had presented the King with four children, of whom only two survived: Marie-Anne de Bourbon, future Princesse de Conti, and the Comte de Vermandois. Louis had made her Marquise de Vaujours in 1666.

After 1674, the "three queens", as they were maliciously called by the Parisians, were only two. With the departure of the Duchesse de La Vallière, the period of careless love affairs was in a sense over. La Montespan was a brilliant woman, both witty and endowed with indubitable charm, but gradually bigotry strengthened its grip around the King. The favourite herself paid the price of this when, on Maundy Thursday, 1675, she was refused communion. Bossuet, profiting from a momentary "religious" crisis on the part of the King, made him promise not to see her again. But charm and beauty carried the day, and the prelate was forced to retire with good grace.

When he wanted something the King was not hampered by anyone. Louis de Gondrin, Montespan's husband, knew this to his cost: he was sent away from Court and several times threatened with prison. La Montespan did not occupy herself with politics. She was content with enjoying the King's favours for as long a time as possible and with drawing from it advantages for herself and her family. The King had two splendid palaces built for her, at which Le Nôtre deployed all his mastery in the arrangement of the gardens and fountains. The ministers and dignitaries of the Court were always ready to satisfy all her whims. It was considered a great honour to be received in her apartments and State officers rendered her homage like a monarch. She moved about with two teams of six horses, wagons full of provisions and a string of servants. Poets and artists immortalised her. Racine celebrated her beauty, the liveliness of her mind and also the off-spring she gave the King. Even the stern Boileau wrote verses to sing the beauty of her eyes and La Fontaine dedicated the second book of his fables to her under the Arcadian name of Olympia. The appearance in the King's life, at the beginning of 1679, of the brief comet that was Marie-Angélique de Fontanges was an omen of La Montespan's imminent disgrace. Marie-Angélique, lady-in-waiting to the Queen, was, according to Louis's own words, as beautiful as an angel, admirable from head to foot, but devastatingly stupid. In the King's life she represents the last moment of frivolity and carefreeness. Capricious and childish, she claimed the right to appear in public at the King's side without being obliged to acknowledge anyone, not even the Queen. The King's infatuation lasted barely a few months and, following a miscarriage which led to ill-health, the young woman was removed from the Court without pity. She died very young, two years later. La Montespan, at the end of the same year, also fell into disgrace when Louis, from now on in a penitent mood, let himself be seduced by Madame de Maintenon, the governess of his children and of whom we will have reason to talk later. The Dauphin and all the numerous illegitimate offspring, were raised in a somewhat

fortuitous way. The King never bothered much with his children, occupied as he was with himself, but finally he grew to prefer the illegitimate ones to the Dauphin, who was often in poor health and was crammed with learned ideas by his governor, the Duc de Montausier. Bossuet wrote for him, *ad usum Delphini,* his *Discourse on Universal History,* a typical example of a biased and distorted piece of writing. The King, perhaps irritated by having a successor already around, kept him away from State affairs for a long time. The others all carried the Bourbon name to the annoyance of the "true" nobles. Louis planned a great future for them at the expense of the French nobility, which had never been sufficiently humiliated. Even *La Grande Mademoiselle* must have given up a good part of her lands to the Duc de Maine.

Versailles

If you look at the feverish activity exhibited in the great labours of Versailles, the Trianon, Saint-Germain, Marly or Meudon, you might think that the King was completely carried away by elation after the Peace of Nijmegen (1678). It was, however, more than that: it was, in a time of peace, the expression – almost the incarnation – of his idea of monarchy.

The traditional residence of the French King was Saint-Germain-en-Laye. Versailles was a swampy plain, suitable only for hunting, where Louis XIII had built a small brick chateau as a summer residence and hunting-lodge. Relatively modest from the point of view of architecture, it is still perhaps the most interesting part of the complex. Very early on, Louis XIV started making modifications and enlargements with the aid of Le Vau, but the great "building fury" only began in 1678. More than twenty-thousand men worked there for at least ten years. The unhealthy air of the site killed off the workers in their hundreds: every night, according to Madame de Sévigné, the dead bodies were carried away in wagons. To that can be added the thousands of soldiers who perished in the fruitless attempt, masterminded by Vauban, to redirect the course of the Eure towards Versailles.

There is something reminiscent of the Pharaohs in this project and in the idea underlying it. Hardouin-Mansart called on all his art to make something majestic and "significant", designing all the architectural lines and buildings to converge on the King's residence. As for Le Nôtre, he placed little temples, fountains, grottoes and arbours around the paths and flower-beds. Meanwhile Le Brun brought sculptors from all over France: hundreds of statues reproduced the Royal features personifying in turn Apollo, Jupiter or Neptune, while goddesses had the features of the King's mistresses – all of them in affected poses in a classical style, somewhat mannered and lacking in vigour.

It is here that the heart of the "ideological significance" of Versailles is to be found. We can see why Louis could not appreciate the powerful genius of Bernini, whom he had none-the-less brought to France, and why he found the "realism" of Flemish painting dull.

The interior of the palace likewise featured only one personality: Louis XIV. The frescoes all took episodes of his *gloire* as their subject. Thus, in the large gallery, both great and minor artists depicted what were frequently insignificant scenes from the King's life in the classical manner. From 1682 Versailles became the official residence of the King and his Court. The King must have needed a lot of patience and self-confidence to put up with seeing himself enlarged in this way on all the walls, whereas it seems that in reality he measured not more than 1.60 metres.

Versailles had cost more than one hundred and fifty *livres*. Colbert was in despair, but the King would not listen to reason. On the contrary, money continued to flow in waves, with the lodge at Marly, not to mention Chambord, Fontaine-bleau, the Trianon or Clagny for La Montespan. At Marly, even more than Versailles, he wanted to realise his obsession with the deification of his own person, surrounded by zodiacs and chariots of the sun. Poor Van Melens wracked his brains trying to find episodes worth the trouble of being depicted. Here also there were the paths, flower-beds, arbours and fountains, the cascades and lakes . . . and a swarm of statues with affected poses and foolish smiles. In the interior, Van Melens glorified the insignificant military actions of the new Alexander.

What was the point of all this? A self-love that was an aberration and out of all proportion (*Deo minor, sed orbe maior* was one of his mottoes)? The Royal pleasure at surrounding himself with beautiful things? Pedantic imitation of great and famous men? It was certainly a mixture of all these, but there is also a clear political idea, however open it is to criticism, of what seemed to be the duties of a true monarch: namely, to confirm the distance between subjects and the monarchy as an institution, to make it served and respected and to leave it to his descendants strengthened by the legacy of great works. There was also a more immediate purpose, linked with the fears and obsessions which constantly recur in the King's behaviour. At Versailles he housed, oversaw, humiliated and ruined the great nobles, whose decentralising tendencies had always been the chief threat to the monarchy. The "divine distancing" of Versailles intimidated forever all the other organs of State, foremost among them being the *parlementaires,* who did not dare to raise their heads again.

Designed by Jules Hardouin-Mansart and decorated by Charles Le Brun, the *chateau de Marly,* was erected in order to enable the King, his relations and a few guests to escape the crowds and rigid ceremonial of Versailles. Pierre Denis Martin portrays it in this painting of 1724 and enlivens its classical perfection by figures of horsemen watering their horses at the fountain in the foreground.

Louis XIV:
Patron of the Arts

Patronage has always been the subtle weapon used by princes not only to "orchestrate the consensus" around their person and their function, but also as a defence against culture and science developing too freely. Louis started by placing the Académie-Française, which had been founded by Richelieu under "Royal protection". In turn he created an academy of sciences, another for medals, inscriptions and *belles lettres,* one for music, an academy of painting with a school at Rome, the royal library, the botanical garden, and so on. All this activity sprang from the King's obsession with glorifying himself and his reign rather than from any love of the arts and sciences. It is impossible to judge from the disproportionate flood of praises and adulation which were, after all, only to be expected, what all this was worth to Louis. However, the result on the whole was what it was bound to be in such an atmosphere where obtaining favour was put before all else: mediocrity in the sciences, and in the arts the appearance of the "preciousness" which Molière denounced so well in *Les Femmes savantes:* the *tartuffes* and the bigots had their big moment. Louis was, however, truly interested, for non-utilitarian reasons, in the decorative arts. He purchased the tapestry factory of the Gobelins, and often visited it, following with interest the various stages of the work. Thanks to this interest of Louis's, Charles Le Brun (1616–1690) found the means of expressing himself. A favourite of the King, in his turn he became a little despot in the art world. The King always gave him a free hand in the recruitment of artists and craftsmen and he brought them from all over France. He was himself a talented painter with taste and imagination. He executed an imposing number of works for the glory of the Sun King. With his pupils, Mignard and Coypel, he deified the King in the field of the decorative arts in the same way as he was being glorified in the field of letters. The century of Louis XIV was without doubt a great period. One need only mention Descartes, Pascal and Molière, but it is also true that the King's despotism eventually led to the extinction of this vein of talent. Historians show us how he

The Academy of Sciences, founded in 1666, is part of the many initiatives in the field of arts and sciences designed to give scope to the obsessive desire for self-glorification of the Sun King. The painting by Charles Le Brun, a detail of which is reproduced here, shows the presentation of the Academy's members to the King.

This anonymous painting dated 1670 represents a scene from *The School for Wives*. Among the principal French and Italian masques known at the time (Arlequino, Pulchinella, Pantalone, Scaramouche, Brighella, among others), the author-actor Molière appears in the part of Arnolfo. He is the first figure on the left.

only brought personalities to notice who were already at work before his accession and how originality progressively exhausted itself. Perhaps it is not entirely the fault of Louis's absolute despotism. The French renaissance indubitably had a peculiar internal fragility to be found both in the rough classicism of Corneille or Racine, in the poetic decoration of Boileau and in the Italianate mannerism of the decorative arts. Nevertheless, these features were definitely accentuated to the point of total vacuousness in the following generation.

La Fontaine, La Rochefoucauld, La Bruyère and Madame de Sévigné escape this judgement thanks to the critical and unfashionable way they portrayed mankind. In fact they simply portrayed what they saw.

As for Jean-Baptiste Poquelin, known as Molière, he deserves a chapter to himself. He was the only person of genius to whom the King granted his protection and even his friendship. Louis XIV always felt threatened by the intelligence of others, but Molière knew how to hide the acuteness of his keen mind behind the appearance of modesty and good naturedness so well, that his

intelligence was forgiven. The King laughed heartily at the misanthropes, the misers, the bourgeois gentlemen and the women savants, since he too despised them. He had more difficulty in saving Molière from the anger felt at *Le Tartuffe:* the Archbishop of Paris condemned the play, the Jesuit Bourdaloue made it the subject of furious rhetorical outbursts, the president of Parliament forbade its performance. However, at this period, thanks to La Vallière, Louis had not yet become a bigot. After five years of agitation and censorship, *Le Tartuffe* was finally performed, to the King's great pleasure.

The King's passion for the theatre was, so to speak, innate. His reign in its entirety, the life of the Court, the ceremonies, the feasts, Versailles even, as well as the wars and diplomacy, was all a long, uninterrupted theatrical performance. The King played the part of himself and he went to the theatre with great pomp, a play within the play, accompanied by all his Court.

Molière died in 1673, persecuted by *tartuffes* even after his death and with him, the only light of authentic intelligence and non-conformism in the King's entourage went out.

The "Réunions"

Louis XIV had a truly exceptional capacity for personally following the business of the State in all its varied activities, and he never forgot foreign policy. Having had his fingers burnt in Holland, he looked with monotonous perseverance for new excuses for injustice. Louvois was always the evil genius behind these enterprises.

Italy was the first objective. In Piedmont, Charles Emmanuel II died in 1675, leaving a minor as heir under the protection of Marie-Jeanne de Nemours. The minor was Victor-Amadeus II. Profiting from Marie-Jeanne's weakness, Louis imposed his will on the country and brought it into the French sphere of influence. In order to dominate the country more effectively he wanted to acquire the fortress of Casale-Monferrato from its lord, the Duke of Mantua. To this end, he bribed the Duke's minister, Count Ercole Mattioli, who, however, informed the Spanish governor of Milan of the deal, which caused the immediate collapse of Louvois's project. Mattioli, captured by the French in 1679, was thrown into prison at Pignerol, then deported to the island of Santa

Margherita and finally imprisoned in the Bastille where he died in 1703.

The republic of Genoa was another important objective. It had been allied with Spain for over a century and its submission to Louis would have enabled him to isolate the Duchy of Milan and to acquire an important bridgehead for the domination of Italy. We have already described the town's bombardment by the French fleet during the Summer of 1678, on the simple pretext of the right of salute. The bombardment in May 1684 lasted at least five days. The whole Mediterranean fleet under the command of the Marquis de Seignelay, Colbert's son, took part and the town was reduced to a pile of rubble. Threatened by a land invasion across the Alps, the town was forced to capitulate in February, 1685, and to accept very harsh conditions which all but destroyed it as a maritime power.

The system of "reuniting" the towns and territories of Alsace and Lorraine with France may have been more subtle, but was just as odious and unjust. Relying on the loopholes in the Treaties of Nijmegen, and even more on his power to intimidate, Louis created *chambres de*

Pierre Denis Martin, *Louis XIV lays siege to Besançon.* After being incorporated in the Spanish province of Franche-Comté, as a result of the "strategy" of the Sun King, the town reverted to France in 1679.

réunion, which were a kind of tribunal of loyal jurists who looked for legal means of affirming the King's "rights" over the towns. The King claimed Lorraine in its entirety, since it had not been discussed at Nijmegen. The *chambres de réunion* of Metz, Besançon and Brisach "discovered" that he had rights over the whole of Alsace as well and even over the Count of Württemberg. Numerous towns submitted spontaneously, the others, such as Solm, Saarbrücken and Lutzelstein for example, were occupied by force.

The annexation of Strasbourg in September, 1681, was the most glorious engagement of all, opening to France a vast zone of influence. The Emperor, involved in a hard war with the Turks, could not intervene. On the same day (30th September) that Louis XIV entered Strasbourg the French troops of Catinat entered Casale-Monferrat, ridding themselves of the Spaniards in return for one hundred thousand *pistoles*.

French pressure was also felt in the north. France did not bother too much with diplomatic niceties, thanks to an ill-considered threat to declare war made by Spain, exasperated by the policy of "re-unions". Some small strongholds fell quickly, but the main objective was the town of Luxembourg which fell after a long siege on 4th June, 1684. Having no misgivings, the King made the most of the grave difficulties in which the Emperor found himself because of the Turks.

On 14th July, 1683, after a series of victories over the Imperial troops, Kara Mustafa arrived at the walls of Vienna at the head of two-hundred thousand men. The city was defended by only some eight thousand inhabitants armed with whatever they could muster. The news stirred up great emotion throughout Europe and, in many countries, armies were recruited to come to the city's aid. Nevertheless, the Viennese had to resist until a Polish army under King John Sobieski and a German army under Charles of Lorraine managed to disperse the enemy at Kahlenberg.

The Turkish advance had been a grave threat to Europe, but although the Pope himself had pressed him to intervene, Louis continued to profit from others' weaknesses to achieve his ends. This was one reason why France found herself isolated in the great conflicts that were to come. Louis's policies had unhappy consequences for the evolution of France.

The Siege of Luxembourg by A. F. Van der Meulen. Fortified after its conquest by Vauban, the town stayed in French hands until 1698.

49

Louis XIV:
High Priest of France

Louis's ecclesiastical policies deserve more than a quick glance. The French Church numbered eighteen archbishops, one-hundred-and-two bishoprics and nine-hundred-and-fifty religious houses (including two hundred nunneries). Despite the reforms of the Council of Trent by way of canon law and of discipline, ecclesiastical positions were not always much more than titles of nobility which went with an income. One often saw young men like Colbert-Croissy, who was barely fifteen, being invested with ecclesiastical office. The dominant influence among the clergy was the Jesuit admirers of the monarchy who, being the instructors, advisers, confessors and preachers of princes, dominated political life and spread doctrinal intolerance.

The King also governed this enormous machine, in perfect agreement with the Jesuits, distributing benefices which the Pope was content to confirm, and allying the clergy to the French crown. Being, as he himself wrote, absolute patron, he had the unassailable right to dispose of both secular and ecclesiastical wealth. Despite appearances, he never concerned himself much with questions of doctrine, although towards the end of his life he was somewhat involved. What interested him was having a united State, obedient to his command. The very idea of an autonomous and dissident minority was inconceivable to him. His concept of absolute monarchy was such that he even opposed some of the Popes (such as Alexander VII and Innocent XI), even going so far as to meddle in the question of infallibility. But his chief obsessions were Jansenism, which was always being revived, and the persistent Huguenot minorities. Jansenism (named after Jansen, the Bishop of Ypres) was an active movement formed to return the Church's pastoral function to pre-eminence and to dissociate it from political power. It wanted a return to religious feeling and moral coherence as opposed to the formalism and laxity of the Jesuits. It gained wide support amongst cultured people through France and this could not be tolerated. Mazarin, as we have seen, dealt it some rough blows, but he had not destroyed it. The King had to concern himself with it once more. In 1674, a brutal decree "deported" the nuns from Port-Royal to Port-Royal-des-Champs, where they were to all intents and purposes prisoners. Four bishops were also accused.

The fate of the Huguenots was much worse. The Calvinist minority, intellectually and economically advanced, had never as it happened caused any trouble. After Richelieu's persecution of them, they had tried to pass unnoticed, while gaining administrative positions and high offices of State. Great industries (forges, paperworks, tanneries, and so on) and numerous commercial undertakings were controlled by the Huguenots, to the extent that they were among the most enthusiastic supporters of Colbert's economic policies. All the same, they were an unpardonable stain on the most Christian kingdom of France.

Perhaps Louis thought along the typical lines of Jesuit morality, that he was doing well in the sight of God in persecuting the heretics. There was, after all, a lot he had to answer for before God. The clergy lent him help and inspiration. The King was surrounded by people like Bourdaloue, Fléchier and Bossuet, who eager as they were to put their intelligence and their pens at his disposal, also promised him religious glory.

But the Calvinists had a still more pitiless enemy in the Marquise de Maintenon, the third and last of the great favourites, whom the King secretly married in the very year of the Edict of Fontainebleau. This edict revoked the freedom of worship granted by Henri IV in 1598 with the Edict of Nantes. The presence at the King's side of this woman, intelligent and determined but distinctly bigoted, made him still more distant, suspicious and vindictive. Originating from a Catholic family, she experienced a brief conversion to the Huguenot faith and thereafter nourished the typical animosity of the turncoat towards her former co-religionists. When she arrived at Paris, poor and scarcely eleven years old, her family saw that she was reconverted to Catholicism. To make herself independent whilst she was still very young, she agreed to marry the poet Scarron, who was hunch-backed and bow-legged and who is remembered in history mainly for his lampoons on Mazarin.

She seized the opportunity to become governess to the bastards produced by La Montespan, whose caprices she put up with for a long time and on whom she avenged herself by discrediting her little by little with the King. With La Mont-

espan disgraced and sent away because of the "poisons affair", which we shall mention later, Maintenon had to put up with the brief period of favour of Marie-Angélique de Fontanges, who was very beautiful but also very stupid and who died at twenty after an abortion. After that, the King was all hers. Taking advantage of the death of Marie-Thérèse (1683), she presented the King with an ultimatum: either she be made Queen or nothing at all. Her progressive rise coincided with a gradual revival of the persecution of the Huguenots. Firstly, collective worship was banned; then under various pretexts the churches of the reformers were suspended. The dignified attitude of the reformers was answered by destroying their churches. During the one year, 1684, more than six hundred reformed churches were destroyed in Brittany, Normandy and Languedoc. There were many summary executions and massacres. All kinds of extremely harsh measures were taken, the most odious being the order to remove all children from their Huguenot parents so that they could be brought up in the Catholic faith. But, as the majority of the faithful resisted conversion, the terrible system of dragooning them was devised. Corps of dragoons were sent into the "rebel" areas and lodged with Protestant families: the violence and abuses they committed are indescribable. Louvois had received orders from the King to act brutally and this he did to excess. After the revocation of the Edict of Nantes, made official on 22nd October, 1685, the persecutions increased. The most atrocious infamies were committed in the course of this operation of conversion by force. Even the Pope, Innocent XI, condemned such ferocity.

Leaving aside the moral point of view, which must be severe and peremptory, the King's obsession was a grave political error: including the victims and the numbers of people exiled, it deprived France of at least two-hundred thousand of its most active and enterprising citizens, who were responsible for a very important part of the national economy, and it brought down the hatred of the whole of Protestant Europe, causing it to form alliances to halt French expansion.

From Grandeur to Despotism

The Other Face of Grandeur: The Subjects

A look at other sectors of public life gives some idea of the intense activity which Louis XIV and Colbert carried on in all domains. In architecture and urban planning, the capital was not forgotten. Broad, rectilinear avenues were opened up and wide spaces were laid out around Royal and civic buildings. The care taken in reconstructing the capital is particularly significant. Paris was, without exception, the most important cultural, commercial and industrial centre in France. She already had the character of an international metropolis, with a large number of merchants and trades from foreign parts. Her population had risen to half-a-million, which was an exorbitant figure for the time.

It is hardly surprising, after the Frondes, that such an explosive concentration of people, should be at the centre of the preoccupations of the King and his minister. In 1671 Colbert confided to his son that all the affairs of State were decided in

This anonymous painting shows *The Louvre and the Seine from Pont-Neuf,* around 1665. The building of the *Louvre* was begun in 1204 under Philippe-Auguste and continued under Charles V, François I, Henri II, Louis XIII and Louis XIV. The palace, which became a museum in 1791, was only completed under Napoleon.

Paris and that all the government's great difficulties stemmed from organizations which were based there. Consequently, he proceeded to perform a veritable surgical operation on the town, breaking up whole quarters and knocking down numerous medieval forts – the strongholds of the people of Paris during troubles. New edifices were built, such as the Louvre, the Tuileries gardens, the Place Vendôme, the Observatory and, on the initiative of Louvois, the Hôtel des Invalides. Nor were the provinces neglected. Wide thoroughfares were built towards Lorraine, Alsace and Luxembourg – with some military afterthought.

Colbert also closely occupied himself with the colonies, which provided France with important

resources. Canada, Louisiana, some of the Antilles islands, colonies in Africa and Pondicherry and Chandernagore in India, were bound by durable links to the homeland. Many Frenchmen found new openings and new perspectives there. As for those who stayed in the old country, more than nineteen million in 1670, they had few reasons to be satisfied.

Louis XIV, according to his own logic, prepared for the greatness of himself and of France and not for the welfare of his subjects who were there only to be regimented, watched over and exploited. The new civil code, introduced in 1667, which speeded up legal proceedings, in fact removed practically all independence from the courts. A few members of Parliament who dared for one last time to protest at this were punished with exile. Justice was in the hands of the King.

He also assumed control of the police, through the means of a lieutenant dependent on his orders. *Lettres de cachet,* simple police orders by which anyone could be put in prison for an indefinite time, began to rain down. With his order of 24th February, 1673, the King finally took all forms of independence from Parliament. He applied the same authoritarian and unjust logic in extorting the money he needed for his great achievements, his wars and his courtly festivities from the people.

Governors wrote to the King, although their words fell on deaf ears, that their provinces were being ruined by the excessive weight of taxes. In 1678, the English philosopher John Locke, travelling in France, noted: "Merchants and workmen give half their earnings to the tax agent... Lands which do not belong to the nobles are taxed and are no longer worth anything . . .". Hunger and misery, particularly in years of poor harvest or bad weather, strewed the roads with corpses.

In spite of this, the *taille,* increased by ten percent, and a whole series of other taxes were levied afresh in 1682. Punishment was terrible also. Troops were billeted on those regions which remained in "debt" to the coffers of the State. Again Locke notes: "A poor bookseller from Niort, who never eats meat himself, boards and lodges two soldiers, to whom he serves three meat dishes a day . . .".

The same year the Venetian Ambassador, Domenico Contarini, an acute observer, wrote:

"Everyone is waiting for something to free them from the slavery to which they have for so long submitted, and they all impatiently watch for events which could change the course of things". His successor, Sebastiano Foscarini, expressed himself even more explicitly and spoke of the "apparent submission of the people, beneath which is smouldering the fire of a revolution". Bloody revolts had already taken place many times in the provinces, for example, at Bordeaux and Normandy. The Breton peasant revolt was particularly violent: they were no respectors of persons and they strung up local nobles and Royal functionaries without distinction from the steeples. The repression was even more violent: thousands of peasants were hanged from the branches of trees. Madame de Sévigné, without otherwise being moved, wrote that children had been roasted on spits by the soldiery. Events did not go any differently in Bordeaux and Normandy. Also, the rebel regions were heavily fined.

It was still the period in which Louis enjoyed festivities. Right from the beginning of his reign he had organised and provided immensely elaborate celebrations. One remembers the tournament of 1662 with the erection of a triumphal arch, but the "pleasures of the enchanted isle" of 1664 and the numerous other festivities in the following years, in which the organisers sought to surpass themselves in extravagance, were even more elaborate. For only one of these festivities, twenty-four thousand lamps were lit. The expense was often of the order of several million *livres* and poor Colbert was beside himself.

During this period the great nobles ruined themselves imitating the King's splendour. But more than festivities, it was with gambling, one of the Court's principal diversions, that they lost their money. Their debts and mortgages taken out on property and titles in order to procure money played right into the King's hands: he had found another means of forcing the submission of the great nobles.

A sympton of the disintegration of this class was its splitting into factions (that of the *dévots,* that of the *temple,* and so on). Even great personalities

Of the three brothers Le Nain, the second, Louis, is considered one of the greatest masters of French realism. The painting reproduced here is one of his most famous works. It represents *Peasants in front of their House.* The "poverty" shown in the painting leaves no doubt as to the conditions of life for the mass of the French people at the time of the Sun King.

LE PORTRAIT DE LA VOISIN.

like Louvois or the Duc d'Orléans were involved. Two episodes are particularly significant.

In 1672 the affair of the "inheritance explosives" broke out by means of which the Marquise de Brinvilliers had committed a long series of crimes, killing her father, brothers and sisters in order to inherit from them. Her doom was sealed by the discovery of letters from her to her lover and accomplice, a certain Saint-Croix. She was beheaded in 1676.

Three years later there was a much more scandalous affair. Catherine Deshayes Monvoisin was arrested and accused of poisoning. All Paris knew her as La Voisin, sorceress and witch. There would have been nothing surprising in the news if numerous members of the high nobility had not suddenly become very nervous.

The sorceress used to prepare philtres and potions for a variety of purposes, but for a few initiates looking for excitement, she would also celebrate black masses, with sacrifices of newborn and very small children. Searches of her quarters did not leave any doubt on that score. She was tortured, according to the practice of the time, and condemned by the *Chambre Ardente,* a court which specialised in witchcraft and which

sat by the light of torches. Although she let it be known that she knew a lot, La Voisin respected professional secrecy and did not talk before she went to the stake in February, 1680.

Her daughter Marguerite, who was sentenced two years later for the same crime, on the other hand, had to "confess". Thus the King found out that La Montespan herself was in the group, that her splendid body had served as an altar and, what was most humiliating, she had had horrible mixtures prepared to stimulate the virility of his Royal majesty. Louis was forced to imprison some of the finest names of his Court, including numerous women such as the Comtesse de Soissons (Olympe Mancini), the Princesse de Tingry, the Duchesse de Bouillon and the Grand Marshal, the Duc de Luxembourg, who was already "under observation" because of his sexual deviations and who was to lie forgotten in the Bastille for fourteen months.

Louis nevertheless tried to reduce the impact of the affair. The ladies were rapidly pardoned and sent away from the Court. Out of the hundred lesser accused, thirty-six were condemned to the stake and the rest exiled or imprisoned for life. These events certainly helped to make the King, who had already fallen into the clutches of La Maintenon, more sombre in character. To this was added the sudden death of Colbert on 6th September, 1683. This was a turning-point in the life and policies of Louis XIV.

Unfortunately, mainly due to the King's thoughtless expenditure, Colbert left a deficit of some millions of *livres,* a State in debt to the tune of several million more and a country crushed by taxes. None of the mediocre personalities who came after him, including Le Pelletier, Pontchartrain and Chamillart, succeeded in managing the finances, which progressively sank into bankruptcy. Colbert died, if not in disgrace, at least in the "divine indifference" of the King, who was annoyed at the continual appeals for moderation in the matter of expenses. Colbert had nevertheless accepted the role of lightening-conductor for the King against the wrath of the people, who hated him even to the point of trying to smash up his coffin during the funeral. His disappearance deprived the King of the only man who could persuade him to act with a little moderation. He left behind him two very bad counsellors: Louvois and La Maintenon.

This portrait of La Voisin, engraved in a contemporary print, is accompanied by the following lines: You were source of great evils, detestable creature / With your horrible poisons you went against nature, / While destiny weaved your despicable stax, / You made death reign for us, and prolonged the Courts day, / But punishment fearful and quite full of shame / Cuts your heinous thread, so you won't live again.

Transformation of the International Political Scene

With the revocation of the Edict of Nantes, Louis XIV completed his programme of subjecting all sectors of public life to the monarchy. However, in England, a diametrically opposed process was developing, which predated the history of the other European countries by several centuries. One can say what one likes about the policies of Louis XIV except that they lacked coherence. Nevertheless, whereas in the early years they were dictated by the necessity of "rationalising" structures that were in the process of breaking up, in later years the King pursued his policies quite beyond reasonable limits. It is not a question, as some historians have remarked, of a turnabout, but of a progressive hardening to the point of mania of his methods and objectives, a mania perhaps accentuated by a presentiment of the "historical defeat" of his example of Caesarism. Holland, which he detested, was livelier, stronger and more Calvinist than ever. And now England was about to be a big disappointment to him.

In England the contest between the Crown and Parliament, begun at the time of Charles I and Cromwell, was not yet finished. The middle classes, active and enterprising, had grown in number and in power, whilst Charles II, with his friendly policies towards France, which were often contrary to the national interests, had lost support for the monarchy. In 1679, confronted by an extremely delicate situation, he had conceded the right of *habeas corpus,* which laid down norms for criminal procedure and protected the rights of citizens. At the same time, Louis XIV was issuing his *lettres de cachet.*

In the years that followed, Charles had to intervene in the struggle between Whigs and Tories, on the subject of the Exclusion Bill which prevented Catholics from succeeding to the throne. The very idea of parties would have been anathema to the French King. For three years Charles avoided summoning Parliament and the party war degenerated into violence and conflict. Charles Stuart died suddenly in February, 1685, aged fifty-five. Tensions came to a head with the accession to the throne of Charles's brother, James II, Duke of York, who had Catholic sympathies. By a succession of unpopular measures,

Philippe de Champaigne, *Portrait of Charles II, King of England.* The last years of his life were dominated by the religious question and on several occasions he disbanded Parliament to prevent the approval of the Exclusion Bill, which would have excluded his pro-Catholic brother James II from the succession.

James succeeded in crystallising a powerful opposition to himself. The Anglican party, having decided to put an end to the King's machinations once and for all, invited William of Orange to come to England. The latter, leaving Holland with more than six hundred ships, landed in England on 12th November, 1688.

Welcomed as a liberator, whereas support evaporated around James II, William put an end to the disagreements without striking a blow. It was indeed a "glorious revolution" brought about by the moderation and sense of responsibility shown by the adversaries. After granting the Bill of Rights, William and Mary were crowned King and Queen of England on 23rd February, 1689. This was certainly the most important event in the whole history of Europe at that period: England set up the first constitutional monarchy of the modern epoch. It was here that a new balance of power between monarchy and Parliament was created. It was the beginning of the two-party system which, by its dialectic, made England a united country and promised a splendid future. It was, however, a distinct setback for Louis XIV, as much for his overall political scheme as for his diplomacy of power relationships. His declared enemy had become the King of his powerful neighbour over the Channel.

The War of the League of Augsburg

Not only had Louis XIV lost an ally, but he had acquired a strong and warlike enemy. William, being himself Catholic, benefited in addition from the immediate support of the Empire, Spain and the Pope. He lost no time in consolidating the great anti-French coalition, of which he was the initiator, called the League of Augsburg.

In fact a state of war already existed. This time Louis's belief in his military power dictated that he should not look to form any alliance. His troops were certainly well enough fashioned not to be "inferior to the largest number", but in the long run the number of his enemies and the number of different battlefronts would prove decisive. Against him he had the Emperor, the Elector of Brandenburg, numerous German princes, Sweden, Piedmont and, finally, Holland and England.

The impatient French forces took the initiative in Spring, 1688. They invaded the Palatinate and shortly captured a large number of important towns. Apart from Cologne and Koblenz, the whole bank of the Rhine from Basel to the Neckar, fell into French hands. Vauban, Boufflers and the Grand Dauphin himself, placed at the head of an army, were covered with glory. Their task was made easy, it is true, by the fact that the major part of the Imperial troops were still engaged with the Turks, but this does not alter the fact that in the course of this war the French troops demonstrated their superiority in the face of a host of enemies.

It is very difficult to understand the reason for this war in the designs of Louis XIV. Clearly, the allies were defending their national interests against an aggressor, but what end did the King of France have in view? Had he a precise objective or was it a question of an abstract "need" for power and domination? The absence of any pattern of alliances (except those with the Turks and the Hungarians, that is to say, the enemies of the enemies, and the violence with which Louvois's troops devastated the Palatinate, which indicates that they were evidently not thinking of making a lasting conquest, make historians lean towards the last hypothesis. Plundering, burning, pillaging, roads and bridges destroyed, castles razed to the ground, Louis's armies reduced the region to ruins.

In mid-October, the French also took Cologne, but despite these favourable beginnings the war promised to be long and punishing. Louis there-

Pierre Mignard, *Portrait of the Grand Dauphin and his Family* (1687). Standing on the right is the first-born Louis, Duc de Bourgogne; in the middle Philippe d'Anjou, the future King of Spain as Philip V, is sitting on a red cushion with a dog on his lap; sitting next to his mother, Marie Anne Christine of Bavaria, is the little Charles, Duc de Berry.

fore tried to weaken the League in another way. James II, who had found refuge at his Court, was persuaded to land in Catholic Ireland to try to reconquer the kingdom of England. He suffered an early defeat against the Protestants of the north at Londonderry, but he stayed like a thorn in the side of William III, forcing him to land in Ireland with one of his armies in the Spring of 1690.

Louis's true enemy was, however, an internal one: financial problems. As usual, he exonerated himself from all responsibility by blaming his ministers. He dismissed Le Pelletier and replaced him with the docile Pontchartrain. One-thousand-and-one new offices were put up for sale and a new lottery was even created, the *tontine;* the handing in of all objects of gold or silver was imposed by decree. Even the King made sacrifices and was imitated by the nobility and the Church: numerous works of art were melted down and destroyed. All this in order to finance a war apparently devoid of purpose.

During this time the armies "covered themselves with glory". On 30th June, 1690, the Dutch of Waldeck suffered a terrible defeat at Fleurus, at the hands of the Duc de Luxembourg, whom the King had meanwhile pardoned for the Voisin affair. On 10th July, Admiral de Tourville inflicted a heavy defeat on the Dutch fleet of Evertsen off the Isle of Wight, under the eyes of the English fleet of Terrington, who was a supporter of James II. On 18th August, having penetrated into Piedmont, Catinat defeated Victor Amadeus II at Staffarde, thus seizing a good part of the country. The capacity for intervention of the French armies and fleet, dispersed on so many fronts, was truly remarkable, but the results, which is characteristic of the wars of the time, were quite out of proportion with the amount of force exerted. The French continued to assert themselves over the next few years, with varying degrees of success. Their command was strongly centralised, whereas William had to "fight with several heads", those of his allies. In order to reward his valiant marshals in a worthy manner, the French King created the order of Saint-Louis.

The invasion of the Dauphiné by Victor Amadeus, who had by now recovered from his defeats by Catinat, brought a new female figure to prominence. Mademoiselle de La Tour Du Pin led the population's resistance, resurrecting the inspiration and the glory of Joan of Arc.

But French power continued to be undermined from within by the disastrous economic and financial situation. The tax collectors increasingly had to make examples of tax evaders by resorting to hangings. Because of Louis's growing difficulties in provisioning his armies and fleets, the fate of the war started in 1694 began to favour the allies and Louis was forced to decide to abandon some of the battlefronts.

His real enemies being aligned along the Rhine and in Flanders, he decided to rid himself of the Piedmont front, on which important forces were engaged without much success, because of the hostile nature of the terrain. He really must have felt himself cornered in having to give up not only Casale, but the fortress of Pignerol, the "gateway to Italy" and the jewel of his father's and Richelieu's policies. The pact concluded with the Duke of Savoy was sanctioned by the marriage of Marie-Adélaïde and the Duc de Bourgogne. Louis could thus concentrate all his efforts on Flanders, where William, now at the head of the allied troops, turned against Namur which was defended by Boufflers. Meanwhile, either to make a diversion or in revenge, Villeroi bombarded Brussels, destroying thousands of houses. On 1st September, 1695, after bloody engagements with Boufflers who could not save it, William took the town of Namur. From then on, this front too had its fate decided. The peace preliminaries were difficult, neither side wanting to make the first move. Sweden, which had taken little part in the war, took the initiative, but there were enormous difficulties with even the allies not agreeing among themselves.

However, on 9th May, 1697, the peace conference opened at Ryswick, a little town near The Hague. Nine long years of war had resulted in France being almost back to the conditions laid down at Westphalia and in the Peace of the Pyrenees. The strangely conciliatory attitude of the King, who had not been defeated in the field, has always astonished historians.

Apart from what he had already been forced to cede to the Duke of Savoy, which was ratified by the Treaty of Vigevano of 1st October, 1696, and which had stipulated the neutrality of the Italian peninsula, Louis XIV restored Lorraine and the Palatinate to their rightful owners, Luxembourg and other strongholds to Spain, and had to grant Holland "barriers" and the usual trade treaty in its

NAMUR PRIS PAR SA MAJESTÉ
LE DERNIER JUIN 1692

S. Le Conte, *The Capture of Namur*. The event depicted was one of the most important of the War of the League of Augsburg. The Sun King was present in person. Little more than three years later, however, the Duc de Boufflers, Marshal of France, had to abandon this important stronghold to the troops of William of Orange.

favour. England obtained recognition of the House of Orange on the throne and compensations in the colonies.

To the French themselves Louis passed off the Peace of Ryswick as an act of magnanimity. Very few believed it, but the peace was a great relief to the French people. The war had been terribly costly in both money and human lives. Henceforth, many could see that there was something unhealthy in a policy of prestige which cost so much and whose concrete results were, at best, mediocre, if not negative.

The King was made still gloomier by the death of Louvois from a heart attack at the age of fifty-six, which occurred on 16th July, 1691. On this occasion, the Royal ego still displayed itself in exemplary fashion: the King received the news with the same indifference as he had in the case of Colbert. He was entirely under the influence of La Maintenon, who demanded to be informed of everything just like a minister, and the King often held counsel in her apartments.

A mystical movement, Quietism, had grown up, and for a time it had the approval of the Pope and early on was supported by Madame de Maintenon, an expert in religious matters. This movement spread widely in France under the influence of a widow, Madame Guyon, so much so that it even counted among its supporters the tutor of the Duc de Bourgogne: François de Salignac de La Mothe Fénelon.

The Jesuits, who were always the first to attack other people's heresies in case they should gain respectability and power, started a war against the movement. Its founder, Miguel de Molinos, was tried and condemned in Italy. Madame de Maintenon succeeded in distancing herself from the movement in time, but Fénelon, by now Archbishop of Cambrai, had to make an act of public submission. Less important supporters were condemned to the stake or imprisoned. Bossuet and the other "ultramontanes", saw their power at the Royal Court reinforced. They were the champions of the rights of Rome and the Papacy against the tendency towards autonomy of the State and of the Church of France. Fénelon, however, went to swell the growing ranks of the opposition.

Vauban himself, a man of integrity with rigid principles, faced with the pitiable condition of the French people, had the courage to denounce the tragic reality in a book, *Plan for a Royal Tithe,*

which gave the actual facts and figures. A Jacobin before his time, he dared to propose the creation of a single tithe, proportionate to income and applicable to all, from the prince to the humblest workman: the book was banned and destroyed in 1707, only a few months before Vauban's death. But such ideas had already been circulating for a long time. In his works *Description of France under Louis XIV* (1695) and *Factum of France* (1707), the *parlementaire* and economist from Rouen, Pierre Le Pesant de Boisguilbert, protested against the absurdity of a fiscal system which undermined the foundations of production and commerce. Among other things he wrote that fifteen million people were in revolt against three hundred who enriched themselves at their expense. Although his works had been published anonymously, he was evidently identified and sent into exile. Still more radical was the conclusion drawn by Pierre Bayle, a refugee in Holl-

In his work, *Plan for a Royal Tithe,* Vauban portrayed here in an anonymous painting, wrote: "From research that I have conducted, I have concluded that one tenth of the population is reduced to mendacity and indeed begs. Of the other nine-tenths, five are unable to provide the first with charity. Three of the four remaining are full of debts and legal suits. The rest, military officers, judges and priests, plus the nobles (and so on) amount to one hundred thousand families at the most".

60

PLATTE GROND DES DORPS VAN JISP

Laurent Scherm, *Commemoration of the Peace of Ryswick.* The four treaties signed by France with Spain, England, Holland and the Empire in 1697, signalled the end of the policy of Catholic unity and universal monarchism pursued by the Sun King.

and, following the Edict of Fontainebleau, in his *Historical and Critical Dictionary* (1696), which was widely distributed in France and according to which reason and religion were not compatible. La Bruyère and Lesage, author of *Gil Blas,* can also be placed among the opposition, an opposition which, even if it did not dare to show itself, was none-the-less both real and profound. In the middle of all this, in the three years which separated the Peace of Ryswick from the opening of the Spanish succession crisis, Louis obstinately continued to prepare for war. Many historians go so far as to think that the concessions made at Ryswick were forced on the King by the conviction that he needed allies, in anticipation of the crisis which was thought to be imminent.

Charles II, the frail and sickly son of the second marriage of Philip IV, whose accession to the Spanish throne had launched the War of Devolution was going to disappear from the scene without leaving an heir. Around his "living corpse" a ruthless race for the succession broke out. The candidates, in view of the complexity of family relationships, were numerous: among them were the Elector of Bavaria, Victor Amadeus of Savoy, Charles of Habsburg (son of Emperor Leopold I) and Philippe d'Anjou (grandson of Louis XIV).

It is impossible to retrace briefly all the plotting, intrigues and deals between the different diplomatic missions and the internal conflicts between the factions at the Spanish Court. Louis XIV really won the day in making Charles write a final testament leaving the throne of Spain and the Western Indies to Louis's grandson. The last descendant of Charles V died on 1st November, 1700. Philippe d'Anjou mounting the throne of Spain, took the name of Philip V. The die was cast and Louis XIV had laid the basis for a new grand European conflict.

The Long War of Pride

It is difficult to say if war was avoidable, France held such an advantageous position; it is nevertheless certain that Louis XIV did all he could to provoke it.

The Emperor, Leopold I, shaking off his torpor, engaged in hostilities in invading Milan in 1701. However, the two maritime powers, Holland and England, showed themselves reluctant to intervene for internal reasons. With the Emperor's forty-two thousand men practically isolated, the picture did not look very promising.

But it seems that the King of France, then aged sixty-two, still had pride and grudges to settle. In the first days of February, he gave the order to occupy the Dutch "barrier forts" of southern Flanders; in one night they were taken and their defenders surprised and captured. Holland, uncertain of English support, preferred to negotiate the prisoners' ransoms, to renounce its

"barrier forts" and to recognise Philip V. Negotiations began at The Hague to redefine the Anglo-French-Dutch guarantees of Spanish Flanders. Louis XIV disdainfully pushed aside all the joint proposals of the Dutch and English; instead he demanded that only the English Ambassador should be present and then only as an observer without the right to speak.

The inevitable consequence was that English-public opinion was offended and the pacifist Tories began to recognise that war was inevitable. They granted William III modest finances to prepare for it. The latter contacted the Emperor and on 7th September, 1701, a grand alliance between the Empire, Holland and England was sealed at The Hague. The game was not entirely played out yet, however. The alliance had a limited character and to begin with did not foresee military intervention.

It was Louis XIV himself who precipitated things and mobilised the English people as if they had

Several naval battles between the Dutch and French fleets took place near the island of Texel, the largest of the Frisian islands facing the Zuider See. This anonymous painting represents the battle of 1694, when the Frenchman, Jean Bart, obtained a splendid victory. Previously, he had served in Holland under Ruyter before becoming Admiral of the French fleet.

been one man, by forbidding the import of English products, mainly minerals and textiles, to France. Moreover, when James II died on 16th September, 1701, Louis recognised his son James III as King of England, Scotland and Ireland, perhaps hoping thereby to divide England in two and relaunch the Civil War. If such was his design, the error was truly enormous and only demonstrated the blindness of his diplomacy.

William, whose anti-French policies had met with so many obstacles, saw his difficulties melt away. He fixed new elections which brought the Whigs to power, although the Tories also supported him. He obtained an army of forty thousand men and one hundred warships and he stiffened the alliances with Sweden and Denmark. However, ill-fortune struck and he died following a bad fall from his horse.

Due to the ill-considered meddling of Louis, Williams' sister-in-law Anne, was proclaimed Queen without the slightest opposition and it was she who signed the official declaration of war on France. For the past year, Olympe Mancini's son, Prince Eugène of Savoy, had been revenging himself and his mother, because Louis had not admitted him to his Court. He retaliated by giving lessons in strategy in the Italian sector to Marshal Catinat and he descended from the Tyrol and pushed the French back beyond the Oglio.

The King found himself forced to replace the powerless Catinat with his favourite, Villeroi, but when he arrived in Italy with a new army, he still did not do any better and suffering a defeat at Chiari (1st September, 1701), had to retire to the French side of the Adda.

The victories of Prince Eugène made a great impression in Europe and broke the invincible image of the French armies. The new found effectiveness of the Habsburg forces greatly contributed to removing the last doubts held by Holland and England. Louis hurriedly sent a third army to Italy under the Duc de Vendôme. A force of eighty thousand men faced thirty thousand and it is not surprising that it succeeded in making things difficult for Eugène, but notwithstanding, in its turn, it suffered a reverse at Luzzara (August, 1702) and had to retire beyond the Adda. During this time, other fronts were opening up. Naturally, Louis's principal objective was Holland. He lined up an army of ninety thousand men against her commanded by Boufflers. On the

Anglo-Dutch side, the command was taken by John Churchill, Duke of Marlborough, an ambitious personality who owed the greater part of his good fortune to his charm and to that of his sister Arabella, who was a favourite of James II; while not exactly a genius of war, he was certainly clever and determined in realising his plans. Instead of directly confronting Boufflers in Flanders, he invaded the principality of Cologne, then turning towards the Meuse he conquered Venlos and besieged Liège, which fell after two months. The French, however, still had a firm hold on Flanders.

The situation was much more complicated on the German front, because of the reciprocal rivalries among the German princes. Bavaria and Cologne were on Louis's side from the very start. Frederick I of Prussia lined up against Louis for financial reasons. Only the Franco-Bavarian occupation of Ulm prompted the other German states, who were united after the Diet of Ratisbon (September, 1702), to declare war on France.

Alsace, in particular, became the theatre of operations and the object of contention. A clash at Friedlingen between the Imperial troops of Ludwig von Baden and those of Villars left the balance of forces unchanged. At the end of 1702, the war was stagnating on all fronts.

The Revolt of the Camisards

The effects of religious intolerance and of economic policies combined to force themselves on the King's attention at a most delicate moment. In the Cevennes there were still important groups of Waldensians surviving and they had recently been joined by many of the persecuted Huguenots. The revocation of the Edict of Nantes had led to an intensification of the policy to convert by force. In 1689 a revolt had broken out which had been brutally crushed. Young people began to travel through the mountains, preaching the holy war. The revolt was sparked off by an episode of hateful and cruel repression. A priest by the name of Chayla, one of the many who, with an escort of soldiers, set out to convert the misguided, having stumbled upon a religious gathering, seized the participants and tried to save their souls by subjecting them to horrible tortures. During the summer of 1702, the priest and his escort were attacked and massacred by the Camisards, so-called because of their custom of wearing a type of short tunic of white linen or *chemise*.

The revolt spread very quickly and involved several thousand men. It was led by a young man of twenty, Jean Cavalier, who was a born commander. In early 1703 before Nîmes, they defeated the soldiers of the Comte de Broglie, governor of the town. The region was nearly in their hands. The King had to deflect his troops and send an army of more than sixty thousand men against them, commanded by Marshal Montrevel. Thus, the revolt began to assume important weight in the international war, as is proved by the fact that Holland and England sent officers to organise the Camisards' resistance. The Camisards succeeded in containing the regular army for a long time despite heavy losses and reprisals. In the single province of Nîmes at least two hundred churches were burnt down in front of the soldiers' eyes and church bells were melted down to make cannons. In reply, Montrevel razed as many as four-hundred-and-sixty-six villages, so it is said, and terrorised the population.

Madeleine de Boulogne, *Almsgiving day at Port-Royal,* tempera. Together with the Huguenots and the Waldensians, the Jansenists – whose spiritual centre was for a long time the Abbey of Port-Royal-des-Champs – were the main target of the religious persecutions enacted by Louis XIV during his reign.

This engraving, by an anonymous French artist of the seventeenth century, shows a group of Camisards taking part in a ceremony. The revolt had flared up after an episode of cruel repression. A priest called Chayla, having surprised a community in the midst of its religious ceremonies had seized all the participants, and "tried to save their souls" by submitting them to the most cruel tortures. During the summer of 1702, the same priest and his escort were attacked by the Camisards and massacred.

Nevertheless, resistance continued and the King had to replace Montrevel with Villars at the beginning of 1704. Villars intensified the repression with massive executions, but at the same time introduced new methods: he split up the army into more mobile intervention units, which struck more rapidly and he promised to pardon any rebels who gave themselves up.

Their situation being militarily untenable, many Camisards defected and Cavalier himself in May, 1704, concluded an agreement with Villars which promised an amnesty to the rebels. Cavalier, on the orders of Villars, was made a colonel and had a regiment formed from his co-religionists.

It was no longer the age of the wars of religion, but although it was anachronistic and destined to defeat, the revolt of the Camisards clearly illustrates the contradictions and internal conflicts of the reign of Louis XIV. The revolt flared up again in the early months of 1705. General Berwick, who had replaced Villars, reneged on agreements and persecuted the religious sects. His suppression of the revolt turned the region into a desert. Cavalier, seized with remorse at the sight of what had happened in his absence, deserted and defected with his regiment into the service of Victor

Amadeus II, Duke of Savoy against the French. This revolt of the Camisards was a painful thorn in the side of France, not only because it kept armies and generals engaged but because it "motivated" the Anglo-Dutch Calvinist soldiers against the Catholic tyrant. Louis, his pride wounded, could not reconcile himself to its existence and gave personal orders to his generals to carry out the suppression without mercy.

France was fortunate in the fact that in the middle of the turmoil of war, more or less all despotic governments are called on to pay for their immoderate use of force. The Hungarians, hardly liberated from the yoke of the Turks, passed under the even more odious yoke of the Habsburgs, who had extended the feudal institutions and heavy taxes of the Empire to them, without any consideration of local customs. Moreover, the old Emperor Leopold was no less intolerant than Louis XIV towards Protestant minorities, which were numerous in this area, and persecuted them ferociously. A violent revolt broke out in 1703. A noble with some Hungarian gipsy blood in his veins, by the name of Ferenc Rakoczy, was its leader. He managed to hold the Imperial troops in check until the end of the war.

The Great Battles

Louis was preoccupied by two other matters in 1703: Portugal and Piedmont defected to the opposition. Both of them had only entered the alliance with France reluctantly since Louis had the bad habit of treating his allies like vassals and they took advantage from his difficulties to pursue their own national interests. Peter II looked on the consolidation of the Bourbon monarchy in Spain with justifiable fear and Victor Amadeus II suffocated in the embrace of his powerful neighbour, who had allied him with the Bourbons through two marriages. The latter, having reached agreement with the Emperor and, despite Louis's sending Vendôme to Italy to humble him, threw himself into the war with such eagerness that the Piedmontese front eventually became one of the most difficult to hold.

Apart from Philip V, Louis XIV's only ally was the Grand Elector of Bavaria, Emperor Maximilian. He therefore conceived the plan of uniting his own forces with his Bavarian ally's and proceeding together against Vienna, which was in grave difficulties because of the extension of the

L. Coblitz, *John Churchill, Duke of Marlborough*. In France, the English General became legendary, not just because of his military feats, but also because of a burlesque song which portrayed him as a protagonist under the abbreviated name of Malbrough.

Hungarian revolt. The plan seemed to have real possibilities of success after Höchstädt (20th September, 1703), at which Villars almost completely destroyed the army of Von Styrum. Disagreements between generals prevented the French from fully exploiting their victory, however, and Villars, who was annoyed, left the command to the mediocre Marsin. The Empire was in grave difficulties. Tallard had beaten the Imperial troops on the river Speyer and retaken Landau. Von Baden was barricaded in Augsburg. Vendôme by the south and Maximilian by the north, had penetrated into the Tyrol. Expeditionary forces, fortified by French money, came from Poland to lend strength to Rakoczy, who had penetrated into Moravia. The Habsburg Empire was in danger of being dismantled.

The old Emperor finally followed the advice of his vice-chancellor, Count Dominik Andreas Kaunitz (ancestor of the great Wenzel Anton), and appointed Prince Eugène as Commander-in-Chief of his armies. The Imperial troops, engaged as they were on three fronts, Italy, Hungary and Germany, numbered no more than eighty thousand men, whereas the army of Marsin and Maximilian alone had one-hundred-and-twenty thousand. Rather than run the risk of a rapid deterioration on all fronts, Eugène decided to concentrate on Bavaria, which presented the most pressing threat.

He came to an agreement with Marlborough on a common campaign. The English General grasped the strategic importance of combined action and gave his full co-operation to the plan. In June, 1704, Marlborough broke camp, excusing himself to the Dutch, who were not party to the secret, by talking of the necessity of a diversion on the Moselle. In fact, he made for the Rhine, passed over to the right bank at Koblenz and proceeded by forced march towards Bavaria.

Eugène and Marlborough met at Grosshepach at the end of June, where Marlborough immediately demonstrated his skill. Arriving at the end of the afternoon on 2nd July before the fortresses of Schnelleberg and Donauwörth, he at once gave the order to attack, without waiting for reinforcements and by nightfall the fortresses were in his hands.

The doors to Bavaria were thus opened to him. Maximilian had to look to defending his own domain and he even began negotiating with the

Emperor with a view to eventually changing sides. But Louis XIV succeeded in reassuring him, promising him important territorial gains and sending to his aid an army of thirty thousand men commanded by Tallard. The French-Bavarian army took up a new position at Höchstädt, where they had been victorious the previous year.

For the first time two great armies, numbering in all more than one-hundred-and-eleven thousand men, faced each other and everyone, whichever side he was on, knew that the stakes were very high, that perhaps the very issue of the war was in the balance. Tallard occupied the right flank, towards Blenheim on the bank of the Danube, with infantry. On the left, towards Oberglenheim Maximilian and Marsin had placed another strong contingent of infantry, and the cavalry was in the centre. The battlefront extended along the Nebel, a marshy river behind which the artillery was posted. The ratio of forces was sixty against fifty thousand, in favour of the French and Bavarians. The army of the allies began to move on 13th August, 1704.

Eugène, having agreed the plan of attack with Marlborough, generously ceded him the command, reserving for himself the most thankless task of containing the French-Bavarian infantry posted in the steep wooded hills of Oberglenheim. The battle raged for many hours without either of the two sides winning a sizeable advantage. Eugène had succeeded, at the price of heavy losses, in infiltrating the left flank of the enemy and taking up a position in the woods, but he had not broken through. In the centre, Marlborough's numerous infantry charges had failed, and he had not managed to cross the Nebel.

At a certain moment Tallard made the mistake of concentrating all his infantry on Blenheim. Realising this, Marlborough stood his ground with a reduced troop and on the contrary threw the mass of his forces against the centre. Until that moment, he had only engaged his infantry against the enemy cavalry, who although they managed to repulse the attacks were beginning to tire. Marlborough continued to intensify the infantry assaults, then in one charge he threw in all his cavalry, even the reserve. The French-Bavarian cavalry, who were experienced troops, tried to resist, but had to retreat rapidly.

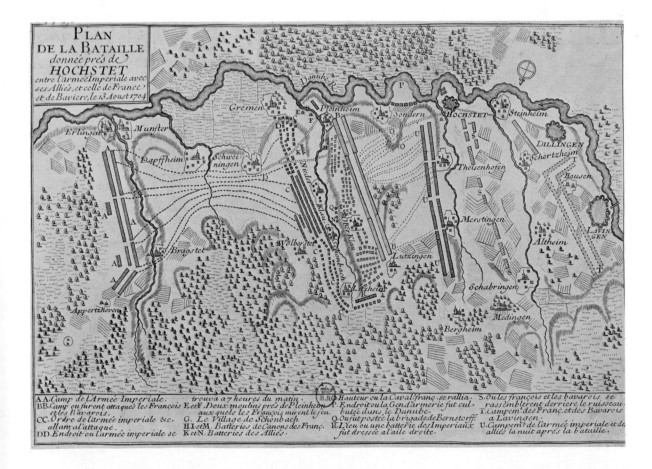

"Plan of the battle fought near Höchstädt, between the Imperial army with its allies and the army of France and Bavaria, 13th August 1704". French engraving of the eighteenth century.

Tallard's right wing, with its twenty-six batallions barricaded in Blenheim, was henceforth cut off from the rest and at Marlborough's mercy. Marsin and Maximilian saved the left wing by beating a retreat. Tallard, bombarded from all sides, had to surrender with nine thousand men, despite courageous resistance. The number of dead and wounded was about fifteen thousand each, which shows the harshness of the fighting. But the military and strategic balance-sheet was, on the whole, distinctly in favour of Marlborough and Eugène. Thirty thousand French were taken prisoner and twelve thousand Bavarians deserted to the other side. The French-Bavarian army no longer existed and with it disappeared the main threat to the Empire. The psychological effects were incalculable. Although the war was to last several more years, this battle set the seal on its future course. At the news of the defeat and the capture of Tallard, Louis raged as never before in his life. What had happened might have led another man to reflect and to reconsider the overall meaning of the war. But the King's pride was above all temporary calamities.

Pierre Mignard, *Portrait of Madame de Maintenon*. Saint-Simon wrote in his memoirs that she "found a King who, having persecuted the Jansenists all his life, believed he was an apostle . . . which made her understand which seed she should throw in the field to reap the greatest profit".

The Stages of Defeat

France did not seize the opportunity either at the death of the old Emperor Leopold I nor on the acccssion of Joseph I to start peace talks. On the contrary, she intensified her military efforts, particularly on the Italian front and the Spanish front where Charles III of Habsburg, who had landed in Catalonia was causing Philip V difficulties. One event which took place in August of the preceding year and which at the time passed unnoticed deserves to be singled out for its future importance in European history: the capture of the rock of Gibraltar by Admiral Sir George Rooke.

Louis XIV did not seem to have any precise plan for the conduct of the war. Dispersed on four fronts, it was intensified here or there depending on where the honour of the King was most threatened. The French armies were still strong and heroically resisting a host of enemies, but the French techniques of warfare were no longer a novelty and thcir adversaries had been imitating them for a long time.

At Ramillies on 23rd May, 1706, Marlborough defeated a strong army commanded by Villeroi and took possession of practically thc whole of Spanish Flanders. At the French Court there were new scenes of rage from the King. It must have been clear even to him that henceforward dcfeats could not be ruled out, but nevertheless his pride and belief in himself encouraged him to persevere: he recalled Vendôme from Italy to reorganise the northern defences of France. In Piedmont, Victor Amadeus II, with little support from the Imperial troops, was practically barricaded in Turin. Vendôme had left and been replaced by Philippe d'Orléans, when Eugène decided to counter-attack. Advancing by forced march by a circuitous route, he succeeded in joining up with his cousin Victor Amadeus in the neighbourhood of Turin on 1st September. On 7th, he decided to attack the French camps between the Stura and the Dora, where the three armies of Marsin, Orléans and La Feuillade were camped – very unwisely as it turned out. The engagement was harsh and for a long time the outcome uncertain, but with Marsin killed and Orléans wounded, Eugène launched a last attack on the centre with the Prussian cavalry and won a new victory. La Feuillade remained a spectator.

In terms of the importance of the force engaged, the Battle of Turin does not compare with other great engagements, but the incapacity of the French Generals, who were fatigued and apathetic, made it disastrous for the army in Italy. La Feuillade recrossed the Alps with what remained of the Piedmont army. Eugène marched on Milan and conquered it. As for the other armies, stationed at Modena and Parma, negotiations began. For Louis XIV, the Italian defeat was the most bitter of all.

In September, 1703, the King had given notice to Victor Amadeus: he sent his cousin Vendôme at the head of an army, to inform him of his wishes; he was left only twenty-four hours to decide. Experience having made him a wiser man, he ordered General Vaudemont to close down the Italian front. The agreements of March, 1707, gave Nice and Savoy to Victor Amadeus, who moreover enlarged his frontiers up to Tessin; the Duchy of Milan and all Lombardy, including the francophile duchies of Mantua and Mirandola, went to the Empire. Capitulation was total.

Spain also had been within an ace of gaining similar advantages. The Portuguese from one side and the Catalans from the other were making for Madrid. On 27th June, the first Anglo-Portuguese expeditionary force of Galway and Las Minas entered the city, and proclaimcd CharlesIII, King of Spain. Only the intervention of a new French army commanded by Berwick succeeded in expelling them temporarily. The situation was slightly better on the German front, where Villars won important successes. However, a new threat to the Imperial troops rearcd its head: Charles XII of Sweden had invaded Saxony. Marlborough occupied himself personally in convincing him to turn his army against Russia (September, 1707). Vendôme, with the young Duc de Bourgogne at his side as his apprentice, reconquered many of the Flemish towns, including Bruges and Ghent, and besieged Oudenaarde. The battle which took place in front of the town is remembered in history because of the unusual way in which it unfolded: the two armies fought without any of the respective commanders giving any orders. The Duc de Bourgogne, unexpectedly caught in the middle of the fighting, gave the order to retreat. It was 11th July, 1708. The thunderbolts of the King, who did not hesitate to demote the best of his Generals, beat down on Vendôme.

Signs of Peace

The King himself began to admit that the state of his finances did not allow him to continue the war. Revolts were breaking out throughout the country and writings appeared on the walls threatening the King with the same end as Henri IV, who had been assassinated.

Numerous Court dignitaries were also in favour of peace. In April 1709 Louis sent the Marquis de Torcy to The Hague to open negotiations, but here the allies, particularly the Dutch, made the mistake of demanding total capitulation, which was not justified by the state of the war. Louis, therefore, decided not to treat any more except on better terms, which is to say after a victory, which was by no means out of the question.

An opportunity arose for Villars and Boufflers at Malplaquet on 11th September. Facing them they had Eugène and Marlborough, who had also decided to finish the war once and for all. The confrontation was very fierce, as one might expect with the balance of forces being ninety thousand for France against eighty thousand in favour of the coalition. The issue was uncertain right up to the end, but the French had to retire although they had fought courageously. Louis proposed new negotiations, which opened in March, 1710, at Gertruydenberg. He had regretfully decided to make generous concessions and to abandon the cause of his grandson, Philip V, but the demand that it should be his own troops which should chase Philip out of the Iberian peninsula was undoubtedly impossible for him to accept.

However, events totally unconnected with the war, allowed peace negotiations to reopen. In England the fall of the Whigs and the rise of the Tories had put the party of peace in power. Also the sudden death on 11th April, 1711, of the Emperor Joseph I, who left no heir, had simplified the Spanish situation, making it possible to see a way to reconciling the different interests. Charles III, brother of Joseph I and chief pretender to the Spanish throne, became Emperor under the name of Charles VI. He was more than ever determined to continue the war and not to give up Spain, but unbeknown to him events were to turn out differently.

On 28th October, 1711, Mesnager for France and Bolingbroke for England signed peace preliminaries, which had been under discussion for some while at the initiative of England. The latter got the lion's share at the expense of the rest of the coalition. Louis XIV emerged with honour, however. Falsified protocols of the agreement were sent to the Dutch, together with threats of a separate peace in case of refusal. After numerous protests the latter had to resign themselves to negotiations, which opened at Utrecht at the beginning of 1712. During this period, with the English having retired, the course of the war became more favourable to Louis. Vendôme, rehabilitated and sent to Spain, had beaten the Imperial troops and the Catalans at Villaviciosa. Meanwhile, Villars in Flanders, had been able to recover a lot of lost ground. On 11th April, 1713, the plenipotentiaries of France, England, Holland, Portugal, Savoy and Prussia signed one of the most important peaces in history, the Peace of Utrecht.

To sum up, England emerged as the true victor: she obtained Nova Scotia, Newfoundland and the Hudson Bay from France and Gibraltar and Minorca from Spain, not to mention the *asiento,* that is to say the trade in negroes and their importation to America. Holland had to be content with merely maintaining her national integrity and only one of the numerous "barrier forts" she had conquered, Tournai. Portugal's right to Brazil was confirmed. Frederick I of Prussia found himself recognised with the title of King and with moderate territorial gains. Victor Amadeus II received the title of King of Sicily, the territory of Montferrat and new territories in the Alps in addition to those he had been granted in 1707. Besides ceding the colonies already mentioned, France had to recognise the House of Hanover on the throne of England and to renounce her rights over Spain, but she did not suffer losses to her territory. The fate of the Empire was also decided at Utrecht in the absence of its representatives: it obtained the Spanish Netherlands, the Duchy of Milan, the kingdom of Naples and Sardinia; but it had to give back Bavaria and Cologne and not least of all it had to concede Spain to Philip V. Charles VI, who felt humiliated by the treaty, pursued the war for one more year, but after some military reversals suffered at the hands of Villars, he decided to sign a peace at Rastadt on 7th September, 1714, which did not significantly modify the provisions of Utrecht. At long last there was peace for the armies and the peoples of Europe.

Eugène of Savoy is thought to have been one of the greatest geniuses of strategy of modern times. Among innumerable victories over the French and the Turks, his triumph in the Battle of Turin stands out. It is depicted here by the painter Jacob Huchtenburg. With his white horse and red coat, Prince Eugène dominates the other figures.

The Death and Heritage of Louis XIV

The year 1711 had seen a great epidemic of small-pox, encouraged by the war. Joseph I had not been the only illustrious victim. In the course of the same month of April the Grand Dauphin, Louis XIV's only legitimate son also died. Even his father did not have many regrets, however; he had shown himself to be both feeble and incapable. He left as presumptive heir a copy of himself, the same Duc de Bourgogne whom we have already seen at Oudenaarde and who had the grace in his turn to die of German measles on 18th February, 1712, a few days after his wife, Marie-Adélaïde. He left two sons, of whom the elder died at the same time and the second mercifully recovered, even surviving from the "cares" of the King's doctors.

Within a short space of time the King saw three generations of his direct descendants extinguished. Some read into this a divine punishment for his conjugal misdemeanours. Louis must have thought so himself because, with the support of Madame de Maintenon, he intensified his religious devotions. He became bad-tempered and shut himself up in a bitter depression. Now that the King was old and embittered, the Royal Court had lost all its charm. In the drawing-rooms, at table, in the immense rooms of Versailles, life went on in hushed tones just as the intrigues of the various factions still discreetly played themselves out.

The King's taste for festivities and banquets had been succeeded by one for liturgical ceremonies in which the entire Court had to participate with as much good grace as possible. One fact, however, must have struck him even more than all the deaths. He had always had a great weakness for Marie-Adélaïde, who had charm and wit, but after her sudden death he discovered in the correspondence that she left that she had been betraying him by regularly informing her father Victor Amadeus of the secrets and military plans of the French. There is no doubt that these family problems also had a part in the King's decision to put an end to the conflict. To begin with he was preoccupied by the question of the succession. The first in line was his great grandson, Louis, who was barely two years old, and he knew from experience the problems which weighed on child kings. The bereavements in his family continued: with the death of Marie-Louise of Savoy, the wife of Philip V, in February, 1714, and a few months later that of the Duc de Berry, Louis's youngest grandson, following a fall from a horse. Inevitably, the Regent for the little Louis would be Philippe d'Orléans, the least loved of all his family, who had moreover acquired the reputation of "poisoner" by his taste for dabbling in chemistry. The King took the decision, which he had been considering for a long time, to confer the right of succession on his illegitimate sons.

On 2nd August, 1714, he handed a sealed will to Parliament, which conferred the Regency on a council of fourteen members; its president, endowed with special powers, would be the Duc de Maine, Louis Auguste, eldest of Montespan's sons. The will was secret and struggles between the various Court factions broke out around the document. They tried to guess its contents by observing the King's favours.

Philippe d'Orléans quickly realised that the wind was not in his favour and, as there was only one copy, contemplated destroying it.

One must say, by way of justification for these base intrigues that an opposition to the "government of the bigots" had grown up around the Duc d'Orléans. Louis had not ceased from persecuting Jansenists for an instant, encouraged in this by a fanatical Jesuit, Le Tellier, who had replaced the pious La Chaise as confessor. In 1709, he had the monastery of Port-Royal razed to the ground and in the last part of his reign he had put pressure on Clement XI to condemn Jansenism. The Pope had given him satisfaction with the famous bull, *Unigenitus* (1713), but now the Royal sleep was disturbed by none other than the Archbishop of Paris, the Cardinal de Noailles, who had dared to receive the bull "in respectful silence" rather than with "warm approval". Intrigues and underhand fighting between the Jesuits and French secular clergy abounded. This was not just a dispute within the ecclesiastical world, but it involved real political factions; on the one hand, the Jesuit intolerance was linked to a Caesarist-Papist

Page 72:
The Sun King used to say his morning prayers in the presence of the Court, as is shown by this miniature taken from the *Hours of Louis XIV,* an illuminated book of prayers; a single copy was made for the King.

This print shows the Abbey of Port-Royal-des-Champs, where in 1674 the Cistercian nuns were deported because of their adhesion to the reforming and anti-Jesuit ideas of Jansenism. On 29th August, 1709, the abbey was surrounded by troops and the nuns dispersed. One year later even the buildings were demolished.

world-view, while on the other, the ferments of religious and moral renewal pointed to a more temperate and "liberal" monarchy. The religious conflict blew dark clouds over the succession.

In the first days of August, 1715, the King's health deteriorated seriously. Violent pains in his legs forced him to stay in bed, from which he nevertheless continued to conduct affairs. A persistent slight fever weakened him visibly and everyone knew that it was the end. The macabre ballet of courtiers trying to snatch final favours from him began, just as they had once tried to do with his father. The Duc de Maine did not hide his intoxication with the power that would soon be his and indulged in jokes and witty remarks. The King appeared calm. Encouraged by La Maintenon, he intensified his religious devotions, gave his last instructions and gave his blessing to the little Dauphin. He died convinced that he had done the best that he could in his "profession of King" (*metier de roi*). Only one thing worried him right up to end: the resurgence of Jansenism.

Some nine million people died covering Europe with blood in twenty-nine years of wars fought mainly to pursue Louis's grand designs. A conservative estimate would be that one million two hundred thousand Frenchmen died; the number of invalids cannot be estimated. At the end of his reign France numbered less than eighteen million souls, while in 1661 the number had bordered on twenty million. If one takes account of the rate of expected expansion in normal times, it seems that at least four million cannot be accounted for. The "technical" cost of the war was one thousand five hundred million *livres*. The human cost, the people's suffering and humiliations, is beyond imagining. Moreover, the King did not feel guilty about this, inasmuch as the well-being of the people had never been part of his programme.

Be that as it may, Louis XIV died at peace with himself, invoking the name of the Most High. On 29th August his condition seemed to improve, thanks to a mixture given to him by some charlatan. Madame de Maintenon had to come back to his bedside; she had already, out of prudence, taken refuge in "her" convent of Saint-Cyr, to which she was nevertheless forced to return in haste on 1st September. The King had gone into a coma during the night and he expired in the early hours of the morning "like a candle". The image is a good one if we think about what followed. At the news of his death, a macabre frenzy gripped France. The people celebrated the event by improvised banquets and by "représentations sacrées" in which effigies of the tyrant were pierced. Here one can see a direct relationship

Antoine Coypel has left this representation of the last official ceremony in which Louis XIV took part: the reception of the Persian Ambassador at Court (19th February, 1715). In spite of what the painter might have wished to indicate, the King's health was irretrievably failing.

between a tyranny and the moral decadence of its subjects. But what strikes historians most is the immediate collapse of his government's policies. This indicates that, at least in his final years, he retained the support of only a few isolated followers who had motives of personal gain in helping to manage the tyranny.

The opposition rose again with violence. The day after Louis's death, the *Parlement,* reunited in full session, annulled the last wishes of the King in the matter of the succession. Philippe d'Orléans, whom he had hated so much, became sole Regent, with limitless powers.

"In order to economise on time and money", writes Drumont in his *Journal de la mort de Louis XIV,* the funeral was rather modest. The people of Paris, who crowded all along the route to the cemetery of St. Denis, vented its rancour, shouting insults and throwing handfuls of pebbles and mud on the coffin.

Drawing up balance-sheets is not easy, for they are always made from a particular point of view, demonstrating the important divergencies between historians according to their nationality or political allegiance. Voltaire was certainly the most enthusiastic and unconditional admirer of Louis XIV. He wanted to see him, perhaps because it served the criticism he made of his own time, as an enlightened monarch, aspiring with all his being to glory and virtue. He made the time of Louis XIV the last of the four great epochs of humanity, the others being the epochs of Pericles and Alexander, of Julius and Augustus Caesar, and of the Medicis in Italy. The judgements of Guizot and of the republican Michelet seem more objective, but in general French historians, even today, always write with a certain understandable dose of nationalism, granting to the reign the distinction of having realised the "cultural supremacy of the French nation". German and Anglo-Saxon historians are much more severe. They tend to see the reign as a contradictory deviation from the institution of monarchy and the ideology of the Catholic counter-reformation. It is still difficult to arrive at an unbiased judgement, because of the very high price which the subjects had to pay for the glory of the King and of France. The terrible financial deficit, the isolation and weakening of the nobility, the multitude of different administrations due to the excessive sale of offices, the heavy taxes which hit the *censitaires* and productive classes in general, were to become the ingredients of the explosive mixture of the revolution in 1789. When the man died who carried it to the summit of its splendour, the French monarchy began to dig its own grave.

The young Louis XV, a few years after the death of the Sun King. He is portrayed here with his uncle, Philippe d'Orléans, who by will of Parliament became Regent of France until the King's coming of age. Philippe held liberal opinions, granted liberties to Parliament and to the nobles, and encouraged Jansenism.

75

Chronology

Life of Louis XIV

1638 – September 5: born at Saint-Germain-en-Laye; son of Anne of Austria, wife of Louis XIII, King of France.

1640 – Birth of his brother Philippe, future Duc d'Orléans.

1643 – May 14: death of Louis XIII; the Queen assumes the regency.

1649 – January 5, the King and Court flee to Saint-Germain, for fear of the Fronde; August 18: Court returns to Paris.

1651 – September 5: he officially comes of age; October: he makes his first journey in the provinces.

1652 – October 21: he triumphantly enters Paris, after the end of the revolts.

1653 – November: he appears at the head of the army in Flanders against Spain.

1654 – June 7: he is solemnly crowned King of France.

1656 – He is attracted to the Mancini sisters, especially Marie.

1659 – Summer/Autumn: he takes part in negotiating the Peace of the Pyrenees at the Isle of the Pheasants in the Bidassoa.

1660 – June 3: he marries the Infanta of Spain.

1661 – March 9: Mazarin dies and Louis begins to reign personally. He has an affair with Olympe Mancini, quickly replaced by Louise de La Vallière; September 5: he has Nicolas Fouquet arrested; November 1: birth of Louis, Grand Dauphin.

1666 – Death of his mother, Anne of Austria.

1667 – War of Devolution. Beginning of the affair with Madame de Montespan.

1671 – Louise de La Vallière takes refuge in a convent for the first time.

1672 – April: he accomplishes the "passage of the Rhine".

1674 – September: Mademoiselle de La Vallière retires finally into a Carmelite convent.

1675 – He begins to wear the famous curled wig.

1676 – April: he experiments as a military leader at Maestricht, but quickly gives it up.

1678 – After the Peace of Nijmegen, he feverishly devotes himself to the building of Versailles, Marly, Fontainebleau, and so on.

1679 – May: Marquise de Montespan sent away in favour of Marie-Angélique de Fontanges.

1681 – Death of Marie-Angélique leaves the field clear for Françoise d'Aubigné.

1682 – He installs his Court at Versailles; Montvoisin implicates numerous persons of the Court including Madame de Montespan herself, in the scandal of the "black masses".

1683 – August: death of his wife, Marie-Thérèse.

1685 – He secretly marries Madame de Maintenon.

1691 – Marquis de Louvois dies.

1700 – November: he has the immense satisfaction of seeing his grandson, Philippe d'Anjou, become King of Spain.

1709 – He is insulted and abused while passing through Paris in his coach; death threats appear on the walls.

1710 – Louise de La Vallière dies.

1711 – April: death of the Grand Dauphin, sole direct heir.

1712 – February: death of his grandson, the Duc de Bourgogne, of Marie-Adélaïde of Savoy, his wife, and of one of his two great-grandsons; there remains only Louis, aged two, who is destined to succeed him as Louis XV.

1714 – May: death of the Duc de Berry, youngest of his grandsons; August 2: he consigns the will which confers the Regency on his bastard son, Louis-Auguste, Duc de Maine, to Parliament.

1715 – September 1: he dies at 8.15 a. m.

History of France

1638 – Since 1635 France has been engaged in the Thirty Years War; April: alliance with Sweden.

1642 – December 4: death of Cardinal Richelieu.

1643 – Death of Louis XIII; Mazarin is appointed first minister; the Duc d'Enghien beats the Spaniards at Rocroi.

1644 – Spring: negotiations for peace at Münster and at Osnabrück; start of the revolt of Parliament.

1648 – August 20: victory of Condé at Lens; August 26: arrest of members of Parliament precipitates the Fronde; October 24: Peace of Westphalia signed.

1649 – Night of January 5: flight of the Court; January 8: Mazarin banished; April 1: agreements of Rueil.

1650 – January 8: Condé imprisoned; the Fronde of the Princes breaks out; Turenne marches on Paris.

1651 – February: Mazarin in exile at Brühl in Germany; September 5: Louis attains age of majority; he recalls Mazarin.

1652 – Mazarin enters France with an army; July 2: Condé occupies Paris; August: Mazarin leaves France and retires to Bouillon (second exile); October 1: Condé proceeds to Flanders; October 21: the King and Court enter Paris.

1653 – February 3: final return of Mazarin; April: alliance with England against Spain.

1654 – June 7: coronation of Louis XIV.

1657 – June 14: Battle of the Dunes, victory of Turenne.

1659 – November 7: signing of the Peace of the Pyrenees.

1661 – March 9: death of Cardinal Mazarin; September 5: arrest of Fouquet, Minister of Finance.

1662 – Purchase of Dunkirk from England.

1667 – Spring: start of the War of Devolution.

1668 – May 2: Peace of Aix-la-Chapelle.

1672 – April 1: declaration of war on Holland; the French army crossed the Lek, an arm of the Rhine.

1674 – Victory at Seneffe by Condé over William of Orange.

1675 – July 27: Turenne dies at Battle of Sassbach; Montecuccoli invades Alsace.

1677 – April 11: a new defeat for William at Cassel.

1678 – August 10: Peace of Nijmegen.

1679 – Peace with Denmark, Sweden, the Empire and Brandenburg.

1681 – Strasbourg and Casale-Monferrato annexed.

1683 – September 6: Colbert dies; Le Pelletier succeeds him.

1684 – June 4: conquest of the town of Luxembourg; August: Truce of Ratisbon between France and Spain.

1685 – October 22: Edict of Fontainebleau.

1688 – Start of the War of the League of Augsburg.

1690 – June 30: victory of the Duc de Luxembourg at Fleurus; July 10: victory of Tourville, off the Isle of Wight.

1695 – Namur falls to William III.

1697 – May 9: Peace of Ryswick.

1701 – Start in Italy of the War of the Spanish Succession.

1702 – Summer: revolt of the Camisards in the Cevennes.

1704 – August 13: Battle of Höchstädt-Blenheim.

1706 – September 7: Battle of Turin, death of Marsin.

1708 – Unusual confrontation in front of Oudenaarde.

1709 – Battle of Malplaquet, outcome indecisive.

1710 – Victories by Vendôme at Briège and Villaviciosa.

1713 – April 11: Peace of Utrecht signed.

1714 – September 7: Peace of Rastadt with the Empire.

1715 – September 1: death of Louis XIV.

Principal Events in Europe

1638 – Western Europe, central Europe and the Baltic sees the bloody Thirty Years War; revolt of the Scottish presbyterians against the Anglicanism of Archbishop Laud; Galileo publishes his *Discorsi intorno a due nuove scienze*.

1640 – Frederick-William I became Elector of Brandenburg; revolt in Catalonia.

1642 – Tasman discovers Tasmania and New Zealand; Civil War in England.

1643 – Torricelli invents the mercury barometer; Sweden under Oxenstierna declares war on Denmark.

1645 – Oliver Cromwell defeats the Royal troops at Naseby.

1648 – Peace of Westphalia; victory by Cromwell at Preston.

1649 – January: execution of Charles I in London.

1651 – Navigation Act of Cromwell against the Dutch; Hobbes publishes his *Leviathan*.

1653 – Cromwell becomes Lord Protector.

1654 – O. van Guericke performs the experiment of the "hemispheres of Magdeburg".

1658 – Death of Cromwell, his son Richard succeeds him.

1660 – England: Restoration of the Stuarts with Charles II; May 3: Peace of Oliva; Malpighi discovers blood capillaries.

1661 – Boyle publishes *The Sceptical Chemist*.

1663 – O. von Guericke invents the pressure-gauge.

1665 – Hooke discovers the cell; Bernini constructs the St. Peter's colonnade in Rome; Grimaldi discovers the defraction of light; Philip IV dies and is succeeded by Charles II.

1671 – Leibniz invents his multiplication machine.

1672 – Newton builds his spectacular telescope.

1673 – Huygens constructs his *Horologium oscillatorium*.

1677 – A. van Leeuwenhoek discovers spermatazoa; Amsterdam: posthumous publication of the *Ethics* of Spinoza.

1679 – England. *Habeas Corpus Act* guaranteeing that no one can be unjustly detained against their will in criminal proceedings; two parties form, Whigs and Tories.

1682 – Halley discovers his comet and predicts its return.

1683 – Kara Mustafa besieges Vienna; the Turks vanquished at Kahlenberg; W. Penn founds Philadelphia.

1687 – Isaac Newton publishes *Philosophiae naturalis principia mathematica*.

1688 – England: William III of Orange on the throne.

1689 – J. Locke publishes his *Letters of Toleration*.

1690 – Locke publishes *Essay concerning Human Understanding* and his *Two Treatises on Government*.

1694 – Introduction to Germany from China of the technique of porcelain.

1694 – Foundation of the Bank of England.

1695 – Leibniz publishes his *Système Nouveau de la Nature*.

1700 – Death of Charles II of Spain; Philip V succeeds him; Charles XII of Sweden invades Poland.

1702 – March 19: death of William III; his sister-in-law, Anne, ascends the throne and declares war on France.

1703 – Foundation of St. Petersburg.

1704 – Sir George Rooke conquers Gibraltar.

1705 – May 5: death of Leopold I; Joseph I succeeds him.

1710 – Leibniz: *Essais de théodicée*; G. Berkeley: *Dialogues between Hylas and Philonous*; G. B. Vico: *De antiquissima Italorum sapientia*.

1711 – April 11: death of Joseph I; Charles VI succeeds him.

1714 – G. D. Fahrenheit invents the mercury thermometer; Leibniz publishes *La Monadology*; England: George I founds the dynasty of Hanover.

Science, Literature and the Arts

1638 – Beginning of the *Dictionnaire* of the French Academy.

1640 – Cornelius Jansen's *Augustinus* gives birth to Jansenism; in Paris there are performances of *Horace* and *Cinna* by Corneille and *The Death of Agrippina* by Cyrano de Bergerac.

1641 – Descartes: *Meditationes de prima philosophia*.

1642 – Pascal invents a calculating machine.

1643 – Molière and Bejart found the *Illustre Théâtre*.

1648 – Paul Scarron publishes *Virgile travesti*.

1649 – Descartes has *Passons of the Soul* printed; Mademoiselle de Scudéry begins to publish *Le Grand Cyrus*.

1656 – C. de Bergerac: *Comic History of the States and Empires of the Moon*; M. De Scudéry: *Clélie*; Pascal circulates his *Lettres provinciales* privately.

1657 – Le Vau begins Vaux-le-Vicomte for Fouquet.

1659 – Molière has *Les Précieuses Ridicules* performed and in the next two years *School for Husbands* and *School for Wives*.

1665 – Molière's troupe takes the title of "Royal Company"; Cardinal de Retz begins his *memoires*; La Rochefoucauld publishes his *Maximes*.

1666 – Boileau: *Satires*; Molière: *Le Misanthrope*.

1667 – Racine: performance of *Andromaque*; Pierre Mignard paints the equestrian portrait of Louis XIV.

1668 – La Fontaine begins to publish the *Fables*.

1669 – Molière "manages" to stage *Tartuffe*.

1672 – Madame de Lafayette: *La Princesse de Cleves*.

1674 – Boileau: *The Art of Poetry*; Malebranche: *Search for Truth*; Le Brun begins work on the Ambassadors' staircase.

1675 – Racine: *Iphigenia*; at the Observatory, Jean Dominique Cassini discovers that Saturn's rings are separate.

1677 – *Phaedra* by Racine and *Phaedra* by Jacques Pradon.

1678 – Mansart, Le Nôtre and Le Brun begin the great works of Versailles; work on the Hall of Mirrors is begun.

1680 – César Pierre Richelet: *Dictionary*; Denis Papin tries out his famous "digester".

1681 – Bossuet: *Discourse on Universal History*; Jean Mabillon: *De re diplomatica*.

1682 – Pierre Bayle: *Various Thoughts on the Comet of 1680*.

1688 – Mansart finishes the colonnade and the Trianon; Fontenelle: *Digressions on the Ancients and the Moderns*; La Bruyère: *Characters*; Dom Perignon discovers the champagne process.

1689 – Racine: *Esther*; Le Brun paints *The Adoration of the Magi*.

1691 – Performance of *Athalia* by Racine.

1696 – *Historical and Critical Dictionary* of Pierre Bayle; Charles Perrault: *The Tales of Mother Goose*.

1699 – Fénelon: anonymous publication of *Adventures of Télémaque*; Roger de Piles paints the entrance to the Academy.

1701 – The Jesuits publish the *Journal of Trévoux* against the Jansenists and the admirers of Bayle.

1706 – Vauban publishes his *Plan for a Royal Tithe*.

1707 – Crébillon stages his tragedy *Atreus and Thyestus*; Lesage: *The Lame Devil*.

1710 – Madame de Lambert opens her "alternative" salon frequented by the young Baron of Montesquieu; in Holland, the *Utrecht Gazette* begins to appear, a journal of refugees from Louis XIV's regime.

1713 – La Motte publishes a free translation of the *Iliad*.

1714 – Madame Dacier: *Causes of the Corruption of Taste*.

1715 – Lesage begins the publication of *Gil Blas*.